UNITY *of* FAITHS

UNITY *of* FAITHS

The Circle of Trust and Hope and Friendship

DAVID KNIGHT

UNITY of FAITHS

Copyright © 2025 by David P. Knight.

All rights reserved.

First published by DPK Publishing—AscensionForYou 2025

ISBN: 978-1914936-25-8 (Paperback Edition)
ISBN: 978-1914936-26-5 (E-book Edition)

All rights reserved and the moral right of the Author has been asserted. Without limiting the rights under copyright reserved above, no part of this publication may be reproduced, stored in or introduced into a retrieval system, or transmitted, in any form, or by any means (electronic, mechanical, photocopying, recording, or otherwise) without the prior written permission of both the copyright owner and the above publisher of this book.

A CIP catalogue record for this book is available from the British library.

The advice or methods found within this book may not be suitable for everyone. It is sold and accepted with the understanding that neither the publisher nor the author is held responsible for the results acquired from the guidance in this 'work'. The author's intention is to solely offer his experiences and wisdom to aid your own search for truth and spiritual development to enhance your emotional, physical, spiritual, and mental well-being. Always seek medical advice from a doctor or physician.

Cover artwork by: 100covers, 100covers.com
Copyediting by: Angela Harders, Paxministries.com
Typesetting and E-book formatting by: Amit Dey, amitdey2528@gmail.com

www.AscensionForYou.com

DEDICATION

God/Source … Sri Sathya Sai Baba … Jesus

And to Issy, Jim, Robert, Kate, Julie, Kimmy, Keith, Jan, Manny, Martin, Linda, and Jill

and for all those who blessed us with their presence …
both in the physical world and those in 'spirit' too.

EPIGRAPH

"I separated Myself from Myself,
So that I may love Myself,
See in Me yourself,
For I see Myself in all of you.
You are My life, My breath My soul.
You are all My forms.
When I love you I love Myself.
When you love your Self,
You love Me."

—Sri Sathya Sia Baba

"Religions are many but the goal is one,
Jewels are many but gold is one,
Stars are many but the sky is one,
Beings are many but breath is one,
Nations are many but Earth is one,
Flowers are many but worship is one."

—Sri Sathya Sia Baba

UNITY OF FAITHS

"Love is My from,
Truth is My breath,
Bliss is My food,
Expansion is My life,
My life is My message.
No reason for Love,
No season for Love,
No birth, No death".

—Sri Sathya Sia Baba

"See no evil,
see what is good;

Hear no evil,
hear what is good;

Speak no evil,
speak what is good;

Think no evil,
think what is good;

Do no evil,
do what is good;

This is the way to God."

—Sri Sathya Sia Baba

TABLE OF CONTENTS

Dedication v

Epigrapgh vii

Introduction xi

Chapter 1: Flowers and Colours 1

Chapter 2: Christmas and Gifts 55

Chapter 3: Symbolism and Colour 103

Chapter 4: Trust and Faith 173

Bonus Lesson 219

Epilogue 225

Further Reading 227

Acknowledgments 231

About the Author 233

Also By David Knight 235

Invitation/Free Ebook 237

Glossary & Spiritual Reference Guide 239

INTRODUCTION

I first became aware of the Avatar of this age in 1999, after some very dear friends went to India to pay homage to the 'man of miracles' ... Bhagawan Sri Sathya Sai Baba. *Sai* is a Persian word used by Muslims to denote a Holy person, and *baba* is Hindi for father. He was a reincarnation of Shirdi Sai Baba, a spiritual master, guru, yogi and Sufi Saint (September 28, 1838 - 15 October 1918) ... who was born on this physical plane on the 23rd of November 1926, and given the name Sathya Narayana Raju. He is affectionately and lovingly referred to as Swami, or simply *'Baba'*, by His devotees.

Sai's message has always been 'not to disturb or destroy any faith', but "to confirm each one in his own faith". Therefore, we could define His mission (and teachings) as transcending religion, through the Unity of Faiths. Amongst his millions of followers were—and still are— presidents, prime ministers, judges, generals, and celebrities. He was admired by both the rich and the poor. Souls were drawn to him because everything he said and did was with love, for love and from love. Through the Sathya Sai Central trust, He founded a large number of schools, colleges, hospitals and many other charitable institutions both in India and abroad.

He visited countries around the world because his 'life was his message'. Sai stated that anyone can communicate with God by turning inward, and He believed that the aim of everyone's life is to merge into the existence of God–liberation. To realize the divinity within, one should live their days with selfless service to others. This principle of 'service to man is service to God' was displayed through the free hospitals, housing and schools that he founded throughout his lifetime.

In 2001, he founded the super-speciality hospital in Bangalore that provided free medical care for more than 250,000 patients! In addition, three main spiritual centres were constructed: 'Sathyam' in Mumbai, 'Shivam' in Hyderabad, and 'Sundaram' in Chennai. He also urged everyone to observe devotional practices and lead a moral life based on spiritual values such as right conduct, non-violence, love, truth and peace.

He demonstrated phenomenal Christ-like power countless times– from varieties of extrasensory perception (ESP) to psychokinesis (PK). Bilocation, resurrections, omnipotence, omniscience, clairvoyance and miraculous healings are considered divine by his followers and devotees, though, of course, he also had critics and disbelievers too.

Since his childhood, Baba had the ability to produce numerous 'gifts' (such as food, sweets, candles, rings, jewellery, etc.) out of thin air, or perhaps from deep within his stomach and out through his mouth for those who were fortunate enough to be in his presence. Perhaps these gifts were the additional 'proof' that they needed to believe?

Devotees around the world felt immense sadness when He left his mortal coil, at the age of 84, on Easter Sunday, April 24th, 2011 due to respiration-related issues. At the time, I could not help but think how apt a day He had chosen to pass.

INTRODUCTION

My own path led me towards Sai many years ago. I had already participated in spiritual and healing 'circles' and meditation groups for a long time. While attending an evening of mediumship in Stamford, Lincolnshire, in t\he UK, I met two wonderful people, Issy and Jim, and they soon became great friends. They were tremendously knowledgeable of the 'spirit' world.

We would try and meet up a few times every month for meditation (and spiritual development work) in Issy's home in Peterborough in the UK. My knowledge and experience in the esoteric fields expanded further. In fact, since my late twenties, I humbly began to receive messages from spirit guides and angels (as well as beings on different realms and planes of existence), mainly through dreams and clairaudience. Larger transcripts came via the psychic gift of channelling and automatic writing from Jesus, and later, our beloved Sai.

In a way, these abilities are simply remembering the connection to God within. I can only describe the feeling as a conduit, directly communicating with 'love and light', and so what is transcribed becomes from 'spirit', through 'spirit', to 'spirit'.

These lessons went on to form a series of published works entitled *I AM I: The In-Dweller of Your Heart* (Parts 1, II, III and 'The Collection'). In essence, they contained spiritual/divine guidance and education on how to transform your life by living in truth, and love, in the modern world.

It was after one of the meditation meetings with Jim and Issy, that they played some of their videos of Sai from their trip to India. It was this very moment, that Sai entered my heart, or perhaps I had simply finally awoken, and remembered, Him! For me, His Divine 'truth' touched my soul and will stay with me forever.

UNITY OF FAITHS

I soon became a devotee and concluded that He was, indeed, God incarnate. (I must point out that following Baba's life and truth hasn't in any way affected my Christian faith). And, although I never went to Puttaparthi–Andhra Pradesh in India to personally visit his temple (*mandir*), I have been beyond blessed to also receive his presence in my dreams and, as you will soon discover, many times during meditation, or when channelling His spoken word. (There are numerous realms of 'reality', so everything that you experience in your head or heart doesn't mean that it is not 'real'. In reality, observing a light 'body' is as relative and tangible as the physical or, perhaps, even more so).

I guess you could say the 'Circle' was formed at this point, with Issy and Jim being the original hosts of the group. Due to an increase in attendees, and the fact that Issy and Jim had both started to become ill, the responsibility of the circle (and venue) was taken on by the lovely Robert and Kate, who also lived in Peterborough. After a while, it became an official Sia Baba group, registered through the Sri Sathya Sai centre in the UK, and which I attended for about ten years.

Unfortunately, in later years, both Jim and Issy had passed away, but Jim's greetings will always stay forever with me. Whenever we met, I'd ask him how he was, and his reply was always the same, "All the better for seeing you." (And you too, Jim. You were an amazing gentleman, so spiritually gifted, and such a gentle soul).

After Issy's cremation service, Kimmy (who was part of the Circle) passed an envelope to me. It contained the following poem that Issy had written one day, after she and Jim and I had meditated together. (Thank you Issy for all your guidance and love and light, I will always remember you. RIP both of you).

INTRODUCTION

Father Almighty,
Thank you for the shelter from the storm, and for the clothes
to keep us warm,
For the birdsong and the trees, for the work done by the bees.
For the food upon the table and for being well and able.
For the world and all the nations, and for your communications.
For your assistance when we fall, and for listening when we call.
For your Son we trust in Him, David, myself and Jim.
Now that this meeting has come to an end, we thank
you again, our Father and friend.
Amen.

The Circle was a real blessing for us all. It was always wonderful to be with like-minded people. (Sai always used to say, 'that good company is important as it cultivates good 'qualities'). Numbers grew, and sometimes as many as twelve people came. We were very thankful that Rob and Kate had such a large lounge! They were fabulous hosts, and their home was always warm and inviting and friendly.

Once a month we'd gather, usually arriving fifteen minutes or so before the 8pm start time. Before the meditation began, we'd catch up with each other's news. Then, Robert would say a short prayer for love and protection, and read a passage from the Bible or sacred text from one of his many books … before we all chanted the divine and powerful, Gayathri Mantra. (In praise of the One Supreme Creator, known by the name Om).

After several Circle meetings, I asked the group if I could read one of the lessons I had channeled before the meditation started. Everyone kindly agreed. I was extremely grateful to be able to share such special information and divine guidance. The reading of a lesson also helped us focus and turn within, towards the calmness of our hearts ... and away from the 'monkey' mind, as Sai used to say!

After the reading, we'd sit in silent meditation for thirty minutes, signalled by the sweet and harmonious chime of a table bell. Bizarrely, this period of time often appeared to last no more than a few minutes.

Once everyone was aware of their body and surroundings once more, each person would send out absent healing, thoughts and prayers. There was a large white Swan's feather on the coffee table, which was symbolic because it is a feather of truth that the Egyptians weighted the human heart—against the truth of their lives. This would be passed around to each devotee, an opportunity for them to share their meditation experience and /or guidance they may have been blessed to receive ... either for themselves or for others in the Circle.

Following this, we chanted the ancient Sanskrit mantra, '*Lokah Samastah Sukhino Bhavantu*' (meaning 'may all beings everywhere be happy and free') and gave salutations to Swami. To conclude the meeting, we would partake in a small amount of *Vibhuti* (sacred holy ash), before a welcome cup of tea and some food treats, wonderfully prepared by Robert and Kate.

Over the years, some participants of the Circle came and went, only briefly dipping their toes into their own discovery for knowledge and wisdom. Other people became the mainstay, where friends soon realised that we were all part of one family of love.

You see, neither your upbringing, work status, age, sex, size, colour of skin or hair, nor your nationality or religion make no difference to God. While in our physical bodies, we all bleed the same. And yet we are also sparks of the Divine, and therefore, when you open your heart and become still for the silence to descend upon you, the voice of truth can be heard.

During one of the early meetings, I was drawn to pick up a pen and paper to become the scribe of the group. It was important for me to record the guidance and education that we were all so humbly blessed to receive. Messages would vary from uplifting individual sentences, to pages of transcript for the group—and to all those seeking permanent peace and bliss.

In this process, my feelings become thoughts, and my thoughts become the written word. However, on many occasions Swami would also appear before us in my mind's eye. And, sometimes, perhaps for protection, Sai Geeta who was Sai's beloved elephant, came along too. (Her name means 'Song Celestial'. In life, she would always trumpet a loud salute ... whenever she sensed Baba's presence). Serenely standing guard, her trunk would gently sway from side to side, shaking unwanted things away, and keeping any negative energy at bay. This is symbolic and apt, because an elephant has profound intelligence. They can hear minute sounds. Remember, hearing the glory of the Lord is the first step to illuminating your path ahead. Sadly, Swami's beloved Sai Geeta passed away ... on the 22nd of May, 2007.

In addition to Swami's visitations, we were sometimes blessed with Jesus's presence, and the lounge would be bathed in a brilliant, white light. Occasionally, they came and stood together before us! The energy and love that filled our hearts, and radiated beyond the four walls, was indescribable.

At this precise moment, I write with mixed feelings: to have experienced such joy and peace and with tremendous gratitude for being a small part of this wonderful group. However, since the inception of the Circle, some devotees/members had passed away. Others were coping with ill health or family issues. These, together with the

Covid pandemic, impacted the group greatly, and it now no longer remains … leaving a void in all our hearts.

It was the pull of my own heart strings that encouraged me to read these meditation notes from many years ago. As I began to feel the power and energy of the words, an overwhelming sensation flowed through my whole being, and I knew instantly that I had the responsibility (and desire) to collate and share them as permanent record of what had taken place.

As a seeker of your own truth, I hope you will find this divine guidance from Jesus, Sai and source/God will resonate within you too … and help in some small way to strengthen and inspire you upon your journey. Everything is from love, through love and to love. You are eternal. You are God. You are Divine, and more powerful (and beautiful), than you could ever imagine!

FLOWERS and COLOURS

Though some members were retired, like the hosts, Robert and Kate ... eight in the evening was a good time before the Sia Baba circle started. Ideal, in fact, for those getting home from work, having their tea and traveling over to Peterborough.

Arriving early, about quarter of hour or so, enabled me to have a glass of water or a quick cup of tea. It would always take me a few minutes to get relaxed. I found it important to try and become focused, and prepared, for the spiritual 'work' that (I hoped) would lay ahead. Some of the group would begin a few breathing exercises, to help to centre themselves and bring calm to the body and mind, too.

Before we began, Robert often said a short prayer of—and for—protection and guidance. In the early years, he would also read a passage of Holy text, such as the Bible, or from one of the many spiritual books he had collected over the years.

I always liked to learn more about Swami's life, and of Shirdi Sai's too. It is said that Shirdi Sai Baba's transformative teachings help to bridge the perceived gap between the earthly and the Divine ... the form and the formless. (As mentioned in the introduction—after a few meetings—the circle kindly allowed me to read a 'lesson' I received, before each meditation started.)

UNITY OF FAITHS

First of all, we all chanted the **Gayathri Mantra:**

"Aum Bhur Bhurvah Suvah
Tat Savitur Varenyam
Bhargo Devasya Dheemahi
Dhiyo yonah Prachodayat."

The mantra has all the three elements which figure in the adoration of God–description, meditation and prayer. The first nine words–

- *"Om Bhur Bhurvah Suvah, Tat Savitur Varenyam, Bhargo Devasya"* – represent the attributes of the Divine.
- *"Dheemahi"* pertains to meditation.
- *"Dhiyo yonah Prachodayat"* is the prayer to the Lord. It is prayer to God to confer all powers and talents. –***Sri Sathya Sai***.

One particular translation of the Gayathri Mantra which I personally like, is from Sir William Jones (1807): "Let us adore the supremacy of that divine son, the god-head who illuminates all, who recreates all, from whom all proceed, to whom all must return, whom we invoke to direct our understandings right in our progress toward His Holy seat."

I read the following lesson: **THE GARLAND**

"Like so many places on the Earth—and indeed throughout creation—I welcome you by placing a garland of beautiful flowers around your neck. To you, it is similar to a radiant rainbow ... but this is vastly different. The petals open wide to the light, resonating from and through and to your heart, and every plume represents truth, love, and hope.

I pre-sent, and now present, this to be adorned by you all—with strength, conviction, perseverance, gratitude, and contentment. So, who will witness these attributes? Who can sense they are bestowed with such a gift? Well, as each body and soul receive it with my grace, only you can answer this question alone. Like karma, no one can erase, accrue, or inflict further imbalance upon anyone else. You all have your own choices to make, and lives to fulfil.

Please understand, the flowers of the garland resemble your souls, connected by an invisible thread of truth. In fact, this is pure, divine, and permanently attached to me … unlike the umbilical cord cut away at birth—or re-birth—separating the body from the mother. No, what I speak of sustains and provides you with everything you need to survive and grow … like a baby in a womb. However, this also carries eternal love, truth, and every ingredient one can think of … and the knowledge of who and what you are deep inside your heart and soul, too.

For many, though, they still imagine isolation, as if divided from me. All must realise … no garland—containing only one flower or symbol—exists to represent division. Nor placed over you upon your arrival in paradise.

Please comprehend the glory of the truth was with you in the beginning, and perpetually stay through you whenever and wherever you reside. Time, distance, levels of vibration or dimension make no difference either. Love is whole. It is universal and all powerful, and forms creation itself. It is not just for the 'Son' but is for everyone. All you need to do is to recognize this through the realization of the self … by remembering and becoming who and what you truly are.

This is the only truth which can be imparted to you in any form or means you can understand. It does not matter where or when you were born into the physical, because colour, creed, and religion bear no effect on your soul. Everything else is for each heart to process when the correct time in your life materializes. Therefore, someone else's truth and experiences may not resonate inside you. Explanations and their own 'reasoning' are more varied and countless, like the grains of sands on every shore, or the stars glistening within the depths of night.

Perhaps you can regard these latest threads as the web of life, a template or blueprint, but ultimately, even these must be digested and acted upon by your own heart. The outcome should be the same. It will lead you into bliss and peace, but this is—and remains—your choice.

When truth is revealed, connecting directly with your soul, you will know and feel it, like a hand in a glove or your feet in well-worn shoes. This is because you have the instant recognition. They belong to you and you to them. They are a perfect fit, comfortable, without resistance or restriction, which brings the sense of wholeness.

Compare this, for example, to a pair of boots, two sizes too small. You would experience pain ... dis-'ease', and immense pressure to persevere and continue wearing them. True spiritual education and guidance are never like this. In contrast, imagine they were way too big. Your balance turns to imbalance, and you will slip and slide about, perhaps even stumble, falling awkwardly to the floor. Truth does not teach this way. So, only you can decide what feels real and ready to be taken on board by your body, mind, and soul.

Of course, there will be those who do not even believe in themselves, and so they cannot acknowledge me either. Perhaps they see the garland of my love in a different light, carrying their own anchor (anger), around their necks, which weighs them down, routing them to the spot. Remember, it is your decision on how you 'see' such things in your life. This has a massive bearing upon events, opportunities, and experiences.

So, do you see your glass half full or half empty? This analogy in its simplest form shows one's thoughts have a major impact on daily life. As this is so, learning to train any wayward or monkey mind is crucial. When a negative thought enters your consciousness, try to override it as soon as possible. Counteract it with positive feelings, picturing an outcome of joy, love, and hope … away from fear, hate, and helplessness.

By recognizing those moments when something bizarre flies into your mind—generating anxiety or stress—it is important to ignore them quickly, and in time, this process becomes easier. The opposite occurs only if we leave negativity to take hold, like a seed which somehow grows upon the infertile ground, yet still flourishes to become a weed. This nuisance must not be allowed to grow. Attempt to pluck and remove them at the earliest opportunity.

One must realise some of your negative thoughts are deep-rooted, and in turn, they take a greater effort to erase. Please try, otherwise they can spread, touching, and taking over others, because your concerns and worries are naturally 'shared' with your family or friends.

Like a common cold, the germination of a virus is quick, does not discriminate over young or old, colour or creed; it only wants to multiply and extend itself. The difference now, though, is that you know you have the choice, a real weapon in your armoury of defence. Let this knowledge be your shield. It will protect you, bringing strength and fortitude over many minor irritations, but even more so, if the roller-coaster of life hits a new low.

Without doubt, you can ride out the troughs and elevate to new heights of experience and happiness, so when all is said and done, try to live your life in joy. I know this can be difficult at times, and you may think it's not much fun or even fair ... which begs the question of how anyone would call the Earth—or life—a 'playground'.

However, the inner connection to each other is eternal, and the garland of my grace you wear will keep you away from all despair ... if you let it! Though I placed this around your neck, it actually rests over your heart. So, reach for it, symbolically, with both hands, to enable your mind, body, and soul to ride those ups and downs with ease. Please enjoy this experience of so-called 'life', as it is freely given to you ... to succeed through love forever. Amen."

After a minute or two, the meditation would start with the chime of Robert's table bell. Baba soon comes into view with beautiful colours swirling around his body. The sound of a trumpet resonates. They seem distant, and yet profound enough to pierce the ether and cosmos. Sai Geeta, beautifully ordained, stands by his side, then strides majestically around the circle. We are protected and know that nothing and no one can keep us from his love.

A white garland of lotus flowers emerges from above, wider than the group. It floats down and weaves between and around us. It quickly pierces through our hearts, connecting us as one. The petals radiate and glow. Their subtle fragrance begins to fill our lungs and cleanse every part of our physical, mental and ethereal bodies.

Swami looks at us all, then seems to glide around the room, pausing in front of Issy. "These petals are for you to blossom. The perfume of your heart will help you to refocus and blend with me." Suddenly, one of the petals turns into a magnificent dove.

"Fly into my heart, dear child. I shall cradle you in my loving arms into eternity. Be at peace."

He turns his body to face Robert and immediately appears before him. This time, the petal within his heart transforms into a large snowflake but also resembles a crystalised star.

"I place this here to reawaken your third eye, illuminating your mind for new knowledge to come. Do not fear the unknown, as I am always near. This life is but a snapshot in your soul's history. I release all negative energy to help you bask in the radiance of truth."

Facing Kimmy, the petals rise towards her throat. "Truth pours forth from the spoken word, light and energy. Through you, allow others to sense and feel as 'one voice – singing in the darkness'. Please listen. Hear the truth, know the truth, speak the truth from and through and to 'spirit'."

I gaze across the room towards Keith. His cupped hands are in front of his chest. Petals begin to pour from his heart.

"The divinity of my heart now resides in your hands. You can caress and keep hold of such a precious commodity, or you can share it. You will always have the choice: love and hold, or love and release. Purity of thoughts and deeds will always follow 'man' in exactly the same way as karma. Live and walk the path of truth, always."

Kate is drifting in and out of her meditation. Baba casts petals from her heart which float and rest upon her crown and stellar gateway chakras.

"Rising like a star, love can shine like a beacon, or it can blend in and feel lost within the firmament above the Universe. I encourage you to stand out for others to notice. Be like the Sun (and Son), so just believe."

Suddenly, the garland between us begins to spin faster and faster until it becomes a circle of light. Time somehow seems frozen, a pause for thought. Swami says, "May love and mercy and God's grace reign eternal, as it is for you all. This is the gift I give to everyone, a reminder of your birthright and blessings through the aeons of time, so continue to shine from your hearts. Peace be with you. Amen."

What an incredible evening for the Circle! Robert signalled the end of the meditation with a single chime of the table bell. We then all chant the **Lokah Samastah Sukhino Bhavantu** mantra:

> *"Lokah Samastah Sukhino Bhavantu,*
> *Lokah Samastah Sukhino Bhavantu,*
> *Lokah Samastah Sukhino Bhavantu,*
> *Shanti, Shanti, Shanti!"*

- *Lokah* refers to the world, universe and every dimension or realm in existence.
- *Samastah* means 'all beings or creatures'.
- *Sukhino* represents happiness, peace and well-being.
- *Bhavantu* is a heartfelt prayer or wish. *Bhav-*the state of unified existence. *Antu-* may it be so.

In essence, this ancient Sanskrit mantra is philosophically and spiritually important. It symbolises a desire that one's thoughts and actions are for peace and happiness and freedom for every form of life, conveying a message of unity and compassion that connects all religions and cultures throughout creation. The power of chanting in Sanskrit is that the root letters and words directly connect with our chakras within and outside of our body. The combination of sounds directs the forces of Creation.

Then we shared in some Vibhuti. After prayers and sending absent healing, we each picked up the white feather to discuss our experiences. Robert and Kate then provided us with some welcome food and drinks, before we started to depart. (I guess you could say it was our *prasad*, our food offered to God). Thank you to our beloved Sai. *Om Sai Ram.*

- *Om* which is the basic but vital vibration from which all creation comes. The whole universe hangs on this primeval sound.
- *Ram* represents the purity and delight inside the heart.

On another evening, we gathered in plenty of time. I had a quick cup of tea and everyone settled down for the Circle to begin. After a brief silence, Robert gave an opening prayer. Then, we chanted the Gayathri Mantra:

> *"Aum Bhur Bhurvah Suvah*
> *Tat Savitur Varenyam*
> *Bhargo Devasya Dheemahi*
> *Dhiyo yonah Prachodayat."*

Then a reading of the Lesson: **RUINS**

"May each heart bear witness to these words, whether read in your mind, spoken out loud, or even shouted from the rooftops! And perhaps they can become etched deep inside you, because throughout Earth's history—and in fact since time immemorial—all impermanent things rot, crumble, and fall into decay. There are no preservatives known to man that will stabilize wood, steel, stone, flesh, or bone into eternity.

Indeed, one may even currently believe the molecules, DNA, microbes, and the like can be frozen in time, but this is not a constant which forgives or succumbs to such notions. Why? Well, it is because life is not one, two or even three-dimensional. The core essence of the soul, once it has left its denser bodily structure, removes the life force and energy which sustained it. All the remaining elements will eventually perish ... even if it takes many hundreds, thousands, or even millions of years.

The reasons I highlight these facts are twofold. First, to make you think about your own mortality. Second, for you to consider the important aspects of your life. In doing so, one can reflect upon what truly stands the test of time and of your eternal legacy.

As stated, many times before, each day you breathe is a gift. However, what you do with it is entirely up to you. Remember though, whether you believe you are alone, or if you are keeping company amongst thousands of people, your thoughts can help others and can carry the energy of love without boundaries or limitations.

One should note, when these are given freely, sincerely, and wantonly, they are most powerful. They shine and rise like a phoenix from the ashes. In contrast, any vibration of anger or hatred and fear tries to destroy the very fabric of structure and order, and one's own self-control may waver.

In the worst scenario, the body would resemble a vehicle grinding to a halt without the oil needed to lubricate vital parts of the engine. One might compare this as being devoid of love. In truth, one has simply ceased to pay attention to one's own body and your hearts and soul's requirements. Comprehend this, 'man' cannot exist without love. It transmutes and encompasses all religions and faiths, every colour, creed, and all life.

Therefore, your own divinity requires devotion, like cultivating a flowerbed. If left unkempt and unattended, it is easy for weeds to bind and suffocate the plants and flowers. Likewise, your divine essence and fragrance will not rise from the plumes and petals of your heart. They become stifled and trapped, thus requiring even greater persistence to remove the negative cause-and-effect scenario. You can achieve this from a helping hand, or by one's own grit and determination. Then, by focusing upon me, you will feel immeasurable power, love, and guidance, but can you—or do you even want to—believe this?

Throughout 'history', countless relics—from many eras—are unearthed. Each tell their individual story. These are links to someone or something's past; and can reveal the way they lived, or even how they were physically 'formed', and then come to pass. Scientists, archaeologists, and historians map precise locations, and with carbon dating, attempt to connect theory with reason, no matter what the season. They endeavour to understand the why, what, and wherefore, to build accurate pictures and assess the turn of events.

In contrast, each of you must grasp the circumstances and situations which unfold in your own lives too, be it on a daily, weekly, monthly, or yearly basis, for they materialize like signposts upon your soul's journey in this lifetime. Every thought, word and deed can resemble crumbs of self-comfort and even pity, or they become seeds of truth. You cast them on and through the ether, but which do you follow? Is it the breadcrumbs of 'desire', or those brand-new paths to explore and shine your innermost light and being?

These choices are your own to make, but guidance is forever with you through your intuition, conscience, and from and through and to those who link with you upon the ethereal planes, and of course those on the 'earth-plane' too.

I also urge you to build your inner defence like castle walls, and even if someone feels or believes they are weak in body or mind, please know, in your weakness, I will strengthen you. I understand your body—but even more so your heart—is under a constant barrage of negativity, despair, anguish, and greed.

Like an army of parasites, they nibble away, attempting to break through, causing havoc and pain. They try to trick your mind, weaken your resolve, and make the walls of truth, dignity, love, and compassion tumble down. Ultimately, such foes appear to stem from beyond the barricades of love, because they have already infiltrated the mind during previous moments of weakness. However, by being vigilant and living life with fortitude and perseverance, you can eradicate harmful tendencies and indiscretions.

So, how can you remove them, whilst at the same time hold new threats at bay? Well, you need to rise above trivialities; forgive another's words, actions, and deeds against you. You can ask yourself if what you are saying, doing, planning is detrimental to another and is befitting of you to be called a human being.

I ask you to fulfil your real potential. You are only ever limited … by your own imagination. By discovering your true self, you will know me. By knowing me, you have self-realization, and through this, discover your own divinity. You will never fear or live in anxiety and misapprehension ever again.

Therefore, appreciate the light is your essence and fortress, and love is all things … the eternal glue which binds you all to me and me to you. It is permanent and can never descend into ruin. Remember, only what appears in the impermanent world in which your body lives can this seem like this.

When humanity realises it is 'one', all the false defences around nation-to-nation, city-to-city, and those between every heart will fall. These will be the only ruins to be 'celebrated' by all, forever and a day. Amen."

On this night, Swami didn't appear before us straight away, but as the meditation started I could feel the sense of his presence around me. Thoughts and words stated to materialise and his loving words began to flow through my pen for each member of the group that were there. Sai wanted to send a brief message to each person.

I looked over to Issy and the garland of white lotus petals appeared through her. "There is only love and eternal peace. No break in the chain …we are forever linked. Remember, I am within and without and I am only a thought or heartbeat away. Call me … I am waiting."

Clockwise around the circle, Julie sat on Issy's left. "Be peaceful. One must rest. I know your prayers. Tasks are set in motion, just go with the flow. Do not let the wayward mind place obstacles in the way of truth. Revel inside the heart and wisdom contained therein. Find me … I do not hide"

I turned my head towards Keith. "Remove hesitation, like a splinter from the flesh. Know a release of pressure or pain is instantaneous. Your energy and love is without barriers or bounds. Therefore, expand beyond imaginary walls or fences. The world is your oyster, so let prayers and love fall where they will."

Looking across to Kimmy, Swami soon relayed his message, "Forget mistrust or hurt. Sometimes another's ego is a test (do not over analyse), live in truth and see the true prize of bliss and peace."

Kate seemed to be breathing more deeply and I knew she found meditation quite difficult. Some soothing words came through, "All you require is focus. Clarity brings true insight. See from and through and to the heart. Simplicity in your thoughts, words and deeds always ... in all ways."

Robert's head was low and was obviously experiencing peace within the stillness. "To journey beyond the mind brings freedom and beauty into your own reality. Likewise, inside your dreams whether travelling across the earth plane or the ether ... simply will it to be so."

I gazed upon the centre of the room. Light, like a spring or DNA helix started to appear in my mind's eye. A vortex of energy allowing truth above and below and within. Sai's face and crown of hair started to encircle us all ... symbolic of oneness. We are whole. A surge of energy, as he began to materialise Vibuthi (Holy ash) purifying and cleansing our minds and bodies. It leaves an imprint on our souls, whilst transforming negativity to positive elements of life.

Swami wanted help us understand a sequence of events: "No birth ... no death ... no beginning ... no end ... no time, for time is eternal. Here I transcend to walk with you, work through you and merge into you. Microcosm and Macrocosm, unity, expansion divine– merging form with the formless. Please receive what you need from my heart to your own. Believe and you will always succeed. Amen." The Circle:

"Lokah Samastah Sukhino Bhavantu,
Lokah Samastah Sukhino Bhavantu,
Lokah Samastah Sukhino Bhavantu
Shanti, Shanti, Shanti!"

FLOWERS AND COLOURS

Robert rang the bell ... thirty minutes had flown by! I picked up the white feather and read the transcribed messages for each devotee, then each person passed it around from left to right, explaining any personal or group guidance that may have come through the silence of their hearts. Following this, came the sharing of Vibhuti ...which is such a blessing. We closed the Circle with a prayer of gratitude, and then sent absent healing and individual prayers. Om Sai Ram/Amen."

It's surprising how hungry you can be after a meditation ... so the drinks and snacks Kate and Robet had prepared earlier were heartly consumed. This was a wonderful meeting, full of *Shakthi* (divine energy) and love and guidance. Thank you dear Heavenly Father/Mother God!.

On another amazing evening, we had all just sat down and became still for the meditation to begin, when a feeling of great tranquillity descended upon the Circle. Robert opened with a prayer and then we chanted the Gayathri mantra...

> *"Aum Bhur Bhurvah Suvah*
> *Tat Savitur Varenyam*
> *Bhargo Devasya Dheemahi*
> *Dhiyo yonah Prachodayat."*

I then read the following lesson: **CLUTTER**

"I am fully aware you know I am here. So welcome to your recognition and connection to our love once more. As you go through your earthbound and physical day, thinking, working, and trying to sustain yourself and your family, one cannot help but see complexity ... instead of simplicity. Sometimes the mind is in such a rush to contemplate, workout, and work through its thoughts, wishes, and deeds, but how many of these are truly required? Do you recognize when 'desire' is influencing your life, which affects those around you, too?

It can be difficult to wade through these matters, as if walking across a desert dune, a sodden field, or worse still, shallow pools of quicksand, as they all attempt to hold and bind you in place. In fact, when one finds oneself in this situation of anxiety and stress, you're sapped of energy, becoming physically, mentally, and emotionally drained.

Please understand, the mind can also bring chaos if left to its own devices and desires. This leads to irrational speech and behaviour. Like tentacles, they try to suck others into the same mire of so-called illusion and confusion. Crucially, one must de-clutter the debris of irritations and trivialities, which endeavours to weave their way into your daily life. Before they can take hold, release the feelings of attachment, in what you falsely sense as being critical to your survival, accumulating what is irrelevant to the body, soul, or heart.

Imagine the scenario of a friend or family member having possessions they no longer need, or that you see material things in a bin, or even items on someone's doorstep with a note, 'free to a good home'. Would you think you actually require them or take them just for the sake of it? Do you desire more 'stuff'? If so, why?

Does the mind tell you this, while imposing a rush of blood to the head? At times like these, stop what you are doing and feel from the heart. Then, simply ask yourself, "For what purpose is this happening? Will it sustain and improve my life, or the well-being of those around me?"

Remember, one can live in a mansion, but you can only fall asleep in one bed. Some, though, assume bigger is better. This is fine, as long as worthwhile, and true reasons exist behind those thoughts and wishes. It is important, therefore, to remove attachment, wherever and whenever possible, in all that's said and done. This becomes simple when one loses the sense of a 'what is mine is mine' attitude or syndrome. By becoming detached emotionally from the material elements of the impermanent world, an easier road lies ahead.

If you can change your thought process, the clutter you collect along the way—in so many aspects of your life—will lose their importance. This enables a clearer passage for your happiness and wellbeing. Of course, I appreciate many people state 'one man's rubbish is another man's treasure', and that 'one day, it might come in handy' … perhaps something will, or maybe it won't.

These statements and traits can be linked to the fear of not having 'enough'. Or one might think it could 'save money in the long run', which is all well and good, but in the meantime, your surroundings remain clogged, with less space for you to move and just 'be'.

In this case, one day you may realise 'you cannot see the 'wood for the trees'. Then, different feelings of frustration, anxiety or even anger can rear their ugly head. The mind and one's health suffer from this conflict within, which affects those close by, such as family and friends, too.

One must comprehend, this is not always about attraction, but detaching the elements which try to cling or hang on to your heartstrings. Retaining gratitude for what one already has leads to appreciation and contentment. Attachment carries the dread of 'losing', leading to worry, anguish and dis-'ease'.

Due to all your different characters, personalities, and responsibilities, I understand one's hobbies are an outlet, releasing a pressure valve, or even a form of escapism for so many of you. We often connect these with sports, nature or even in the materialistic sense, whereby you collect something. You name it ... stamps, music, books, pictures, ornaments, thimbles or toys, and someone, somewhere, has a fascination and needs to store or accumulate it.

Why do this? Is it wrong, or right? Well, everything carries a reason for each one of you. Remember, all you do must be good for yourself and society. So, does it harm or propose any forms of conflict to oneself or another? If you gave it up or stop right now, what thoughts do they trigger deep within you? Inside, you'll know the answer!

Whatever you do, realise by clearing and removing any clutter—on any level of your being you can think of—will create 'space' ... yes, room for both the true you, and 'us'. Perhaps new ways of thinking and being, and new opportunities can finally flow to and through you without certain aspects of your current life getting in the way. How good would this make you feel?

In addition, so many people and 'things' in your life will come and go, like the ever-flowing ebb of tides upon the Earth. So too, your emotions keep a 'push me - pull you' effect on them, through your everyday choices, concerns, attitudes, and so-called happy and sad times. Remember, the only thing you need is love, and to love 'self', each other, and all life.

Appreciate your possessions may indeed become a cause and trigger of a memory, but ultimately, whatever touches your heart needs no actual physical reminder. Love is the only permanent issue here, and this one truth shines above all transient elements in every dimension, time and space which has ... or ever will ... exist.

It cannot be boxed and stored away in a shed, garage, or attic. Nor can it be destroyed by fire, be buried, or disappear into the ether, although time can appear to make the 'need' and link seem to fade. But true love is the jewel in our crown, for it radiates, resonates, and never dissipates. You can find this, I promise you! Like a needle in a haystack of concern and trepidation, the beautiful plumes, and petals of a single flower amongst the weeds growing in barren soil, or a four-leaf clover seemingly disguised within countless of its kind.

Try to remove sentiment, for like cement, it attempts to bind you. In doing so, the false attachment is removed and 'sent to me' instead. I retain it as my burden and not your own, because you no longer need to rely on it. You will feel freer within your life; this I assure you.

All that is required for you to do ... is to decide where and when you will start. Is it in the mind, the heart, or in the very room in which you read or hear these words? Appreciate I am always with you, so even if you believe certain aspects of truth are difficult to achieve, lean on me.

Ask me to help you move forward, and I will give you strength to accomplish what you must complete. Just believe and trust in yourself too, for you can make the changes you need in your life.

When all is said and done, everyone must accept their most prized possession—the physical body—has been removed ... but will soon appreciate they are left with the perfection of light, love, and soul. Through self-realization, you can attain pure bliss and peace and know the true removal of clutter. Amen."

We all sat for a few minutes ... and let the reading filter through our minds and into our hearts. Robert gentle rang the table bell as I readied my notepad and pen to record (and then share), Sai's following guidance.

Swami appeared before the group. He stood in the ceremonial white ... yet wore a garland around his neck and shoulders which resembled a beautiful rainbow, colours more vibrant than anything I had ever seen. Sai Geeta lifted her powerful trunk and like a trumpet announcing His arrival whilst bringing protection and strength and power to all physically and spiritually present.

His right hand waved like a wand producing Vibhuti immediately. The captivating perfume of violets and lavender filled the air as the sacred ash poured over our heads to cleanse and purify our thoughts. A tremendous glow of happiness seemed to ooze from Swami's smile, "My blossom of my heart now envelops you all. It is our union." Time seemed to freeze, encapsulating the moment.

Standing before Kate, he plucked a flower from the garland for her. "Pink for love and a symbol of our oneness. May these petals float into your heart, so the perfume of your own divine essence radiates and transcends the physical body. Remember, Love all ... Serve all."

Turning to Issy ... a brilliant yellow rose manifested itself from the garland and gently fell towards her. It appeared to hang in front of her forehead, suspended by ethereal threads of knowledge and wisdom. "I provide this for enlightenment and a determination to succeed. Your pathway will be lit by the Sun/Son and become much clearer. Know that in the journey ahead, I am with you always in every way. Trust in me ... we are 'one'."

Julie was sitting on Issy's right, the head of a flower, a purple delphinium appeared to radiate around her while her face glowed within a soothing gentle haze. "You receive this expansion of spiritual and mediumship gifts. Become energized by the power which flows through you and all life. Energy to assist you in guiding others towards their goals, and highlight the truth far beyond where you reside is imminent. Preparation for this 'work' ahead has already taken place. Believe in yourself always."

Keith was next. The rainbow garland around Baba began to spin at an incredible speed and soon became white light. A flower resembling a carnation shot out of this incredible energy into Keith. "Purity and clarity of thought and heart will encapsulate your heart and soul. Embrace the light at every opportunity. Shine for others … to help them follow their own truth within themselves."

Baba turned towards Kimmy and as the garland slowed to a halt, a large blue hydrangea fell into her hands. "Like the seas, you are a wave that merges upon the ocean of my love, so let our love be carried from shore to shore. Guide those who live in fear to the safety of my loving arms … the harbour of rest and eternal peace and bliss."

Jan's head slightly lowered as Sai moved towards her. She became bathed in an amber/orange hue. A beautiful Dahlia seemed to sit on her crown chakra. "Like my usual coloured gown, I envelope you with the fabric of love within time and space and all creation. The thread connects my heart to yours, entwined forever. Live in the knowledge that you are never alone and you can always call upon me until the end of time."

Manny received what I can only describe as a green ball! (A Dianthus Barbatus–perennial plant?) Surrounded with brilliant green aura, Swami spoke," Let nature embrace your thoughts and feelings.

Allow the beauty of the world shine through your heart. All life is precious. May your love reflect this nurturing aspect of human existence towards all those you meet. Everything is connected and nothing is wasted. Be joyous in every aspect of your life."

Sai finally turned to Robert. The flower dropped from the garland … a vibrant red Geranium. "Light shall rise like the phoenix from the ashes. I empower you to take flight within your hopes and dreams, so that the knowledge and experiences you receive are shared. May they light the way for other's … away from the shadows of doubt and fear."

Swami's energy and form began to dissolve before me. And just before disappearing he said, "Live in love always." The meditation had come to an end … precisely as Roberts chime of the bell. Divine timing in more ways than one! We gave absent healing and salutations to Baba.

"Lokah Samastah Sukhino Bhavantu,
Lokah Samastah Sukhino Bhavantu,
Lokah Samastah Sukhino Bhavantu

Shanti, Shanti, Shanti!"

After passing the white feather and discussing our experiences, Robert shared some Vibhuti with us all. We had been truly blessed by Sai's presence and divine guidance and presence once more! After some snacks and cup of tea, we each made our way home. Om Sai Ram/Amen.

Spring was on its way, hoorah! It was a little earlier in the evening as I drove to Peterborough, and I couldn't help notice the sporadic patches of vibrant yellow daffodils that lined a bank of grass just outside a village I was passing through. This certainly lifted my spirits, as I had felt a little down after a long and hectic day at work. Little did I know … that flowers and colours were to be prominent to our beautiful Circle/group once more.

We all greeted each other and mentioned how mild it felt. (It's a typical British trait to regularly discuss our weather, ha ha). Robert and Kate provided a welcome drink and we all sat down to get comfortable and ready for what 'Spirit' had planned for us. An opening prayer was said before chanting the mantra:

> *"Aum Bhur Bhurvah Suvah*
> *Tat Savitur Varenyam*
> *Bhargo Devasya Dheemahi*
> *Dhiyo yonah Prachodayat."*

Lesson. **CREATION**

"When you are sad and your heart feels separate from me, you imagine I am distant in some way, shape, or form. So, I request that you, your family, and your friends—or indeed any living thing within Creation—do not feel this way ever again.

You may try to question why these notions of isolation should even enter your mind, but the answer to these issues is, for one reason and one reason only, 'attachment'. Coming to terms with—and accepting—the need to 'let go' is a crucial part of educating your heart and soul, so I will explain more about this shortly.

Remember, while there are those who become aspirants of truth, most people do not seek the genuine purpose of living or being.

Therefore, they only see an occasional flash of inspiration and knowledge. However, no matter what level one thinks they've reached, if you live upon the 'earth-plane', there are always lessons to learn.

In addition, whilst the acquisition of the material and wealth exists, such desires will constantly smoulder and burn within the individual and the masses. However, the accumulation of money—or anything else—is not wrong or harmful, unless an attachment to it radiates more brightly than the love you actually are.

Subsequently, it becomes easier to follow a path of bondage and discontentment, because of a misplaced craving and the belief these things will quench a thirst or fill the 'belly', when in reality, it simply occurs from fuelling a negative flame. The devotee, and the aspirant/seeker of truth must therefore rise above these issues whenever they can, but do not misconstrue what I now explain.

People often seek me in the same way and somehow need to reattach themselves. As stated earlier, I am not separate from you, and am in front, behind, above, below, and on the outside of you, so how can I be out of reach? After reading or hearing this, you may now think I must surely be 'within' you too, and yes, this is partly true, but in truth I am all of you—your whole being, everything. This becomes much easier to understand when you pause and consider me as 'creation'.

Each night, millions of souls will gaze upon stars, galaxies, and the firmament above them, only to gasp in awe at such beauty and magnificence. Meanwhile, scientists, scholars and academics—throughout the eons of time—all contemplate the 'big bang' and evolution, continually wondering how, why and when it all started. However, if you can appreciate the simple and straightforward statement of 'I am all things', then you must be everything, too.

Once again, do not try to find me in faraway places. Just remember, I am the wind upon your face, the water you drink, and the ground you walk on, too. Hence the universe, which lies beyond your mind's perception, is only a reflection of my love, my body and my being, and hence, what you sense, see, feel, touch, hear, and taste are all one of the same.

So, if you were to continue with this train of thought, you may wonder if you were really 'born' at all, and did you manifest as a soul by some magical potion? The answer is, of course, no. Therefore, as you are light, you have not gone away or come from the light. Your true essence cannot be filtered or watered down because you are whole ... and only your own false realization can trick or deny this to you.

With so many attitudes and misunderstandings concerning creation, it is vital that you realise and find out your own beliefs and thoughts about this reality. In this process, you should not abandon any religion or spiritual practice which seeks truth ... nor offer me flowers or fruits in gratitude for my love and support, as I do not require such things.

It is far wiser to honour and love the real you and be true to your own divinity. This is the course and path all must learn to take, so do not even believe I attached you to me, as this is a false and misleading 'need', which wells up within you. By loving yourself, you will love the truth inside, and openness, trust, faith, and many other qualities will manifest themselves through, too, and from you. Know that this is true creation in action.

I appreciate many people will read this text and still wonder about evolution and the manifestation of life and energy, matter, and anti-matter, and so on and so forth, but please return to simple thoughts and understanding. For instance, when your tears fall, does the well of your heart run dry? No. Upon death of your body, would you suddenly become closer to me? No, because you are neither separate, divided, near or far from me.

I ask you to have faith in yourself and acknowledge this truth, and then you can truly flourish, becoming a brighter and more vibrant being and soul. In addition, you will grasp who, what, and why you 'are', and this will reveal you can move forward with increasing devotion and deductions in your goal. Only your karmic debt and your life's choices can slow you down, but even these can be swept away by living in, with and through right conduct, as a human being and a real part of the world's society.

We are one, and so there cannot be any dispute or confusion arising over the concept or words of 'what is mine'. Everything 'man-made' is perishable or impermanent, while life existing through love is immortal and everlasting. Do you realise and comprehend this? Indeed, you can make things happen, joyful or otherwise, you only need to believe!

Trust in me, for I am here for you all, and know every heart, mind, and soul. Therefore, please understand there are no secrets you can keep from me (I am I); and you cannot hide, just as you cannot hide from yourself. Try then to be happy and content, and yet strive to achieve and express your inherited gifts, too.

Know the reservoir of my heart is always full, and it flows to, through, and from you. I want you to ride upon it, like a crest of the wave, enjoying the journey to the shore of eternal peace and tranquillity.

Believe me, when I state you have such a special opportunity in this lifetime to step off the rebirth treadmill, so do not even wait one or even 1000 new lifetimes. One must find me by finding yourself. All life is but the size of my fingernail, and yet your love is more powerful and beautiful than you could ever imagine. With this known ... light up the path within your heart and complete your very own creation! Amen."

Robert's table bell chimed for the 30 minutes of silence to begin. Shortly after the meditation started, energy and light and colour filled the room. Swami stood in the usual place near the fireplace. Petals and blossom began to swirl above us ... encircling us with His protection. I sensed a musical 'tuning' fork in the centre of the room, which resonated at a certain pitch and brought subtle tones of peace and harmony to all hearts and souls both physically, and spiritually, present.

I humbly gazed upon Baba's face. He was smiling and radiated joy. "Let the colours bloom. Allow the fragrance of love fill your hearts and be shared with all in truth. May each colour and petal perfume the road ahead."

He turned towards Manny as various shades of blue descended from flowers above. " I provide light blue to help you keep cool when being tested. And dark blue–like the oceans–to help you remember you are but a wave upon the sea of love. Ride the waves and peaks and troughs with equanimity. Peace surrounds thee."

Jan: "Pink is for love ... and the aroma which fills your heart and mine as one. Let it flow where it will, for you are already free. Love retained equals nothing gained. Love shared proves you care. Love received always strengthens thee. So you sow ... shall you reap."

Kimmy: Yellow seemed to gently shower down upon her. "Droplets of the Sun/Son fall like stars and comets across the night sky. Each illuminate the horizon and provide hope for all who bear witness to the celestial and universal magnificence. This light paves the way forward ... just embrace and take a step upon it."

Kate: All shades of purple glow over her body: "Petals like violets are Heaven 'scent' ... radiating around your being, filling your aura with tranquillity and peace. Wherever you go this is with you. Others will receive the words from your lips, your thoughts from your mind, and be touched by your actions and deeds."

Julie: A vibrant red hue fell over her. "Rose petals softly fall from my crown to create a new path for your journey ahead. It will become smoother, flow naturally. Do not force things, allow the notion of this to be your guide in the next phase of your life. Just 'be'. Trust in the knowledge all will be as it should be."

Robert: "Orange petals fall upon you, a reflection of my gown. Like citrus fruits I am the vitamin and essence so drink the truth of love. Become nourished in body and mind and soul. Because our hearts are 'one' ... how can there ever be any deficiency or lack of what you need?"

I observed Sai raising his right hand as if to wave goodbye. H then said, "Live in joy and peace, always." Once again, as if precisely on cue, the meditation came to an end with the chime of the bell. We concluded an amazing evening with individual prayer and absent healing and salutations, all feeling tremendously humbled and blessed. Circle:

"Lokah Samastah Sukhino Bhavantu,
Lokah Samastah Sukhino Bhavantu,
Lokah Samastah Sukhino Bhavantu

Shanti, Shanti, Shanti!"

After a couple of minutes, meditation messages were discussed, with each devotee holding the white feather in turn. Robert shared Sai's sacred ash with us, and then Kate invited us all to partake in the food on the dinning table. I helped to make the hot drinks with Robert and Kimmy. After another twenty minutes we said our goodbyes ... and I was already looking forward to our next Circle! Thank you again beloved Swami. Praise be to God. Om Sai Ram/Amen."

Unfortunately, it was a couple of months before the next meeting. The middle of summer and the warmer evening meant that the drive over to Peterborough was most enjoyable. I'd often see many Red Kites where we lived. They are beautiful medium to large birds of prey. They have a reddish-brown body, a forked tail and have a distinctive call. That night, they seemed to appear from nowhere ... and it felt as if they are following me!

Over the years I have come to trust (and believe) they are Swami watching over me, wherever I go. One must understand that he is no eye (I) in the sky like 'big brother' ... one who spy's on your every move ... but the universal mother/father who provides constant love and protection.

We had all arrived early which was great. It's always nice and relaxing to have a drink beforehand. The start of the meeting took its usual format ... opening prayers, salutations to Sai, and chanting of the mantra:

UNITY OF FAITHS

> *"Aum Bhur Bhurvah Suvah*
> *Tat Savitur Varenyam*
> *Bhargo Devasya Dheemahi*
> *Dhiyo yonah Prachodayat."*

Lesson: **MIRACLES**

"Oh, my 'son', my heart, and my love ... we are 'one', and no life form or energy can divide, separate, or cut us in two, as everyone is whole and already complete. All must comprehend this in order to progress into and beyond the truth, for while many souls take baby steps into this reality; humanity could leap and bound towards everlasting peace. Please remember, I do not criticize anyone in my endeavour to educate those who are unsure of their higher self.

People can experience tiny nuggets of information and spiritual knowledge in a variety of ways; some are uncommon, whereas others materialize through the expression and creativity of the spoken word, or via books and films, etcetera. They may not tap into their golden heart of love and light at this time—or wish to—but appreciate that it is here and here alone, where the unwavering certainty of truth will sink deep within their core. Eventually, wisdom follows the acceptance of the one true miracle ... the undying beauty, bliss, and Nirvana of both you and me.

This surpasses all creation, because the tiny plumes and flames inside your physical heart are 'me', the source of all things. However, you cannot see these through sight alone ... as they only become visible when the eyes of the heart, mind, and soul are in unison. As this is so, everything else is impermanent, forever dying, and being reborn.

In contrast, the permanent Atma—your divinity—and light within you can never fade and die and is as beautiful and majestic as it has always been. Only the layers of sticky black molasses (caused by your karma), betray and falsify the truth. So, unless the individual body removes these through good conduct, right action, and with love, then one's true being remains blinded—both consciously and subconsciously—until they make small and more frequent changes.

Please appreciate, someone can change this very second, or it may take countless years to comprehend the why, what, where, and who they are. However, no one needs to wait for yet another life, and become 'reborn' into physical embodiment ever again. This choice is available to everyone, so who will take up the challenge in which all hearts have set for themselves?

Each person can achieve their heart's desire and make their ultimate dream come true, but will you? By keeping me near, dear, and by wishing to know, feel, need, and love me, then I remain a reflection of those wishes. Remember, I am not distant from you, so why do you try to distance yourself from me? I am not just behind, in front, or beside you, but I am inside you because I am you. By recognizing me, you will simply recognize yourself.

Think for a moment about your family, friends, and pets. Perhaps they are the centre of your life. Here lies a special bond of love, alongside compassion, togetherness, and trust, and many other qualities expressed between you, too. However, even though these links and relationships are especially important (because they help you grow and flourish as a human being), do not be afraid or unsure of what I am about to tell you.

This is all attachment. You may think you love your dog for your dog, but you do not … you love your pet for yourself. You believe you love your wife, husband, son, daughter, father, and mother for them; but no, you love them, somewhat selfishly, for yourself, and inevitably, this causes anguish, heartache, and pain. Therefore, how do you love unconditionally, and be able to 'let go' without grieving when they depart the mortal plane?

Well, when you can appreciate their essence cannot die, and your knowledge, experiences and understanding of what and who you really are makes sense, the penny will finally drop! Once you know me 'within', then the answers to such queries become simple. In fact, true love, light, and wisdom are not complex. It is simplicity itself ... so please comprehend and follow this through your heart and life ahead.

Hence, the real miracle of my love is 'you'. Love is everywhere, love is who you are, and who and what you will always be. Remember this eternally, for even in your darkest hour, I am there because I love thee.

Then, when you are still and in silence, you will recognize me as the air filling your lungs, the breath of life. When the sunshine falls upon your face, know I am here, there and am forever in every place. Should you hear bird song (like a gentle lullaby), realise I am within you always, never to say goodbye.

When you smell the fragrance from colourful blooms and petals, understand I am the only scent perfuming your heart. By bearing witness to spectacular and natural phenomena, know your gaze has seen but a fragment of my power. If you touch and wipe a tear from your eye, appreciate your soul bleeds the truth of your real 'self' that is both you and I.

Therefore, please let the resonance and vibration energies of peace continue to shine and grow and try to overcome negative feelings and false emotions; by stopping them in their flow. By continually becoming 'still', you partake in the sweetest pill ... no Pavlov's dog, no false or hidden pretence, only truth to sustain, help and guide you. Always follow your heart, and in doing so, you will know mine. Love and light go to all, and all go to the love and light … remember? Amen."

We all settled down for the meditation to begin. Soon after, I picked up my pen as Swami appeared before me.

"Hello, my dear children. You gather here because your hearts are drawn to me. Like silk threads, you form my gown of truth. Each are connected, inside and outside and from and through my heart. Yes, we are one. As such, I provide my love for each of you. To protect, guide and teach and nurture the reality of our light and destiny. Be at peace always. Your father, mother, sister, brother, and friend, for all time. Amen."

Kim: "Regarding your knitting needles, wool, colours and patterns … I urge you to keep strong and have faith and design your life through your thoughts and words and deeds. Think of 'mother' and the expression 'knit one … pearl one'. Here the lesson is patience."

Keith. "Like the strings of your guitar, pluck up the courage to change what you feel you ought to. Each decision (important ones) will strike the right chord inside your heart, so do not fear and do not 'fret'. My love … like a sweet lullaby, will soothe any troubles from your brow. The lesson for you is to feel the love.

Kate: "Just like Joseph and his coat of many colours, do not concern yourself with the minds constant dictation for (or of) a palette of choice. Let your heart be the colour that flows onto the canvas or paper. As a rainbow crossed the sky, let the same energy mix both truth and light. Oil and water do not blend however, and likewise, one's reality can become stifled when anxiety or fear try to be at the forefront of your mind. Let it go, and always go with the flow. Here, the lesson is one's clarity of thought."

Julie: "Holidays can be joyous occasions … different places and different people. They say a change is as good as a rest. But, wherever you want to go or be … delve deep into the well of your heart, and you can experience exactly that. Remember, to let go of the mind. Follow your intuition, those gut feelings … those little nudges and reminders that I am forever watching over you. You are free. The lesson here is life is a journey of discovery of your true self."

Robert: "Age before beauty or so they used to say. Do not worry or concern yourself as the body ages and tires. All you can do is to try to do your best in every area of one's life. I do not give marks out of 10 for results achieved, but elevate your soul to greater heights of knowledge and truth, because of effort and commitment and perseverance. Lack of will is not part of your makeup. In fact, remember the Lord's prayer and the line, 'May thy will be done'. The lesson for you is to simply allow me to work through you."

Just as the bell was due to chime and indicate the end of the meditation … Swami was about to turn and leave, but stopped. He spoke again, "May all those who have gathered here today, within and beyond the four walls of this house … understand I am within, without, above, below, beside, in front, and behind every step you take. I am you and you are me. We are indeed 'one' into eternity. Amen." Swami raised His hand, then disappeared.

Wow … if someone was previously in doubt of Sai's blessings and grace then surely no longer! That was truly a magical experience. Beloved Swami, thank you so very much from all our hearts. We each sent out absent healing. Then, Robert concluded the evening with prayers and salutations, before our partaking of Vibhuti. Circle:

"Lokah Samastah Sukhino Bhavantu,
Lokah Samastah Sukhino Bhavantu,
Lokah Samastah Sukhino Bhavantu

Shanti, Shanti, Shanti!"

Kate had prepared some food treats along with a nice cake she'd baked. These were soon devoured as we shared meditation experiences and messages while holding our special feather. With the light and warm evening, we stayed a little longer to savour the internal and external nectar Sai had provided us. Praise be to God! Om Sai Ram/Amen.

We all looked forward to tonight's Circle, especially after our previous meeting and divine guidance we'd received. After our greetings and a welcome drink, we settled down for the spiritual 'work' ahead. I had a sense of profound peace. The energy of the room felt so calming. It is always wonderful to be with like-minded and light-hearted friends. After opening prayers the group chanted the mantra before the reading:

> *"Aum Bhur Bhurvah Suvah*
> *Tat Savitur Varenyam*
> *Bhargo Devasya Dheemahi*
> *Dhiyo yonah Prachodayat."*

Lesson: **SOMETIMES**

"When all around you seems to pass you by—at what feels like a million miles an hour—sometimes you just need to 'be'. I bear witness to each day rolling into the next, with one's 'chores', duties, and those responsibilities of work, family, friends (as well as the home) which insist your attention. Life can be a constant rush or blur, with the mind engaged and ceaselessly thinking of the next minute, hour, day, week, month, and year ahead.

So, just for a while, can you place the exterior on hold, pressing an imaginary pause button upon the day's tasks, in order for some 'time-out'? I do not—and will not—encourage the waste of any second or minute, but explain that within the stillness of your heart, one can re-learn and experience each new day. One can chose to feel more alive, and in doing so grow to know thyself (and I) in greater and more meaningful ways.

Do not be dismayed (or disturbed) by lists of things to accomplish or problems to solve, people to meet, places to go, or by the inconvenient sounds made by 'man', or man-made impermanent things. Try to de-clutter the mental horizon.

Focus instead upon nature, and those natural sounds around you … like birdsong, insects buzzing, and the rustling of leaves. Or, if you should open your eyes, try gazing out towards passing clouds and those birds in flight, and the butterflies and bees resting on nearby flowers. You could even go outside … to feel the sunshine on your face. It will surely lift your spirit and cast off many burdens from your shoulders.

Please also understand, true peace reigns not in the time between wars, but in the letting go of everything you think or feel you were, are, or can ever become. So too, just as I have stated before, if you wish to 'enjoy', then simply end your search for 'joy'.

Realise and appreciate most people who strive to feel happy require the next thrill or so-called 'high' from sensory pleasures, but these are only fleeting. One then has to deal with the periods of time between them. However, by treating pleasure and pain with the same indifference, no angst or depression can set in. The after effect of excitement will simply drain away and disperse, like water through a sieve.

In contrast, within moments of contemplation—along with periods of togetherness and harmony between family and friends—peace stays constant. It remains captured like a photograph, becoming etched into your heart and soul forever. These are the special times, and the energy and vibration of their essence, one can remember and cherish more easily.

Appreciate your love and my love is one which permeates all things. It is everlasting. So, how do you come to know and live this? Well, first, you need to recognize it. For example, imagine the fragrance of a flower, and by doing so, you'll understand you do not need to see or touch the flower itself to experience this. Simplicity is the key, and it must always remain this way, remember.

You understand the difference between night and day; dark and light, wrong or right (unless the mind is impaired through or by the body) don't you? As a result, all life knows the source of love deep within, and hence, love knows all.

Love is the only permanent thing in all Creation. So, why must you worry almost every day? The world keeps spinning, the sun will continue to shine, and the rain will fall, and where life is born, it inevitably dies. Indeed, the period within physical embodiment is brief. Only your love, character, and personality will leave traces across the sands of time. These cannot fade, unlike the memories of those who are still earthbound, as they remain a part of you, your soul, and very being.

Understand and believe too, we are all connected. We cannot be separated by the exterior illusion and confusion which surrounds—and wishes—to invade what you think is your personal 'space'.

It is only by making a conscious effort to grasp who and what you are—and can yet become through self-realization—that enables you to experience true stillness and inner growth in silence.

How many times have you ever said aloud, "I can't hear myself think in here", citing noise, loud talking, or music? It is the same with listening and conversing with each other. Can you really hear me when your body or mind is forever engaged in work or play?

Therefore, when you're inside the stillness, you will feel, sense, and also know the answers you seek. This will become more clearly defined than ever before. Believe then that I am waiting for you. I am ready at all times, for I am within, without, beside, above, below, and am everywhere and in everything. Hence, you become able to trust me to always provide you with whatever you need (but not necessarily with what you think you want … or when).

Please, do not wait for 'life' to become just a little too much to bear before you seek me—as so often is the case through fear, pain, or loss—because you can call to me when you feel happy, relieved, and are glad, too! Life always continues. Therefore, acknowledge and look forward to those times when everything around you needs to carry on, but you (as if disappearing from everyone else's view), must sometimes, just simply 'be'. Amen."

With a brief chime of the bell the meditation began. The notepad and pen was ready by my side. In the centre of the room a circle light formed very quickly, and Baba wearing his orange gown soon appeared. Flower petals showered from His hand with the sweet perfume of His divine essence. "Allow the aroma of my love fall where it will. Each colour resonates perfectly to meet your needs– spiritually and mentally and physically. Let's begin …"

Keith: Pink–"May my love encapsulate your whole being. I bring the softness of my embrace to wear away all traces of ego within man. I perfect your thought and words and deeds ... but your divine light and soul need nothing as you are already whole. I urge you to remember this and continue to believe yourself and me. Peace."

Kimmy: Yellow–"Daughter of light, bright yellow petals wash over your mind and alleviate the worries of the day. Like the daffodils, allow the freshness of spring brighten each day and lighten the load of one's concerns and cares. Continue to walk forward in truth and peace with my blessings."

Kate: Purple–"Vibrant energy envelopes you to support and strengthen you when you feel 'down'. Take each day as it comes. I am within you and besides you always. Be confident and self-assured in the knowledge we are one ... together forever. So, never, ever feel you are alone, the energy I send will lift your mind and lighten the weight upon your mind and body and soul."

Julie: Blue–"Shades of blue from the sky and sea will cool all fears and concerns. I am the bridge over the emotional waters which sway back and forth upon your shores. Understand, you are the vessel that can never be lost, not to me. I am the breath of life which steers you through the uncharted voyages and earthly journey. I shall direct you ... you simply have to trust."

Robert: Orange–"These petals that flow from my gown now assimilate your heart to mine. No division, no separation. I am the nectar of life that helps to define your purpose and goal through thought and words and deeds. Express the love from within your heart with a smile or touch of the hand. Simplicity is the key. Life is love ... love is life. Each day can become what you make it. Create and live in the truth of you."

UNITY OF FAITHS

As the meditation ended, Baba smiles and waves. Once again there are swirls of colour. Petals still flow to and from his hand and heart. He seems to elevate away within a rainbow, yet somehow remains present, watching over us all. Circle:

> *"Lokah Samastah Sukhino Bhavantu,*
> *Lokah Samastah Sukhino Bhavantu,*
> *Lokah Samastah Sukhino Bhavantu*
>
> *Shanti, Shanti, Shanti!"*

Absent healing was sent followed by salutations for Swami's blessings and grace. I then shared the amazing guidance Sai gave for us all while partaking hot drinks and nibbles. Praise be to God. Om Sai Ram/Amen.

It dawned on me a while ago, that part of what each member of the circle received—in terms of 'colour' and subsequent guidance—from Swami, appeared to have a direct correlation with their current thoughts and emotions. The advice within each person's message could easily sooth our feelings and assist us in any circumstances throughout our lives. Therefore, one must conclude it is divine and universal and timeless. Any person could easily browse these pages and discover a line or passage that resonates inside the heart or mind …or both.

On this particular evening, it was apparent that Sai wanted to leave us in no doubt, that He is here for us all … encouraging and supporting and protecting and guiding and loving us in all ways, always. We settled down in our seats and became still, before the Circle began with the mantra:

"Aum Bhur Bhurvah Suvah
Tat Savitur Varenyam
Bhargo Devasya Dheemahi
Dhiyo yonah Prachodayat."

Lesson: **DEBRIS**

As the connection between love and light guides the pen, I now welcome you with these thoughts and words. Please comprehend the ink, which glides across the page, is only an impression made in wet sand. Therefore, will the teaching of such lessons remain within your heart and soul, or blur and fade, washed away by the tides of your emotions?

In all sacred texts and 'written word' throughout time, every consonant, vowel, phrase, sentence, paragraph, and book, resonate at their own frequency. Because of this, their understanding remains fixed, resembling deep-rooted trees, or they float like feathers and leaves upon the breeze. Therefore, if one's vibrational state matches the energy of what they read or heard, then the information, knowledge, and wisdom become easier to digest, as the recognition of truth falls into place.

In contrast, sometimes the young or old—no matter what their colour or nationality—will place it to one side until a new day dawns. Everything has its time, place, and purpose, so an individual's learning cannot be forced or rushed ... wisdom arrives precisely when it is meant to. If this were not the case, it would be like a new-born baby studying for a degree or scholarship.

All spiritual guidance and education work this way, and the seeker, aspirant, devotee—or whatever name you care to place or describe this search and quest for truth—will realise this. Every one of you is resonating and working on different levels of transition within your hearts, minds, and souls … but one cannot say they are any better or have progressed further than another.

Appreciate too, the current bodily incarnation you each possess is not affected in this way. The soul resonates and illuminates, not by another's thoughts or actions, but of its own accord and power within. It is the same with all karma/karmic debt. As such, your brother, sister, mother, father or any other next of kin cannot erase or clear past deeds carried out by yourself.

One could call these things your soul's debris, the fallout from the illusion and confusion over many millennia. This takes a persona of many forms and guises, and along with bruised egos, there is the physical, mental, spiritual, and ethereal pain, or someone who displays a spoiled character and personality, a real Jekyll and Hyde.

Even so, things differ from previous generations, and those eras of time, which drifted by upon the 'earth-plane'. This is because I give you an opportunity and a gift—from my heart to yours—and during this 'age', every being and soul, across billions of worlds within time and space, can all reduce or erase what they require inside.

Simply put, through your own self-realization, you can attain your eternal happiness and joy. This is no game of pretence, by somehow brushing the debris under a carpet, or trying to disguise the truth of past lives or deeds. No, this is permanent, for I place my loving heart around every spark of divinity to cleanse the negativity, angst, fear, and pain from the plumes and flame of your true self.

In this moment, bliss and peace will shine eternally, allowing you all to witness and experience my love. The tears of your soul will cascade like crystal waterfalls throughout my kingdom ... knowing that love reigns supreme, formed in recognition that you are born of love, remain free by love, and forever will be loved.

Many call such events 'ascension'; this is fine, though this indicates a 'coming from' and a 'going to' scenario. In fact, you already are, were, and always will be part of me ... in whatever form or appearance the soul takes. Try to comprehend, the soul has been magnetized because of the bodily senses and lack of mind control. This attracted debris over the passages of time, by false fear, desire, hate, anger, jealousy, and so much more from misguided and trapped negative thoughts, words, and deeds.

Through your endeavours and expansion of truth and light, the polarity will change. The acts of compassion, forgiveness and joy dissipate and transform negativity across time and space, and through love, a shift across the Earth's population will alter from selfishness and doubt to selflessness and a certainty we are all one.

Your frequency of divinity will radiate like iron filings upon a piece of paper, and I am the new magnet which attracts you in waves of rainbows and colours more beautiful than you could ever imagine.

Understand too, I am the pot of true gold that awaits you all, but you do not need to use any man-made appliance to detect where I am, though you must still dig deeper than you have ever tried before. No spades or shovels are required ... only the quest for your own truth inside you. When you know thyself, you'll know me. In knowing 'I am I', you will appreciate all of creation is at your disposal and should be used.

No matter whom or where you are, understand this opportunity knocks for you all. Please trust in yourself, and therefore trust in me—as I often reiterate to you—because each burden of your incarnations, I will bear for you ... but do you believe me? Do you think I can do this for you? Is a leap of faith really required when you fully comprehend that I am all life? You alone must answer this question.

It is important to comprehend your reality in this lifetime. If you cannot, or do not wish to change or grow—within the light—I shall not forsake you. Your soul's path—which you set—will continue, of course, because, as always, these choices are your own. Some may wonder or beg to question, "Well, why bother with this so-called opportunity or amnesty then?" I reply and simply state, I love you all ... and by using earthly connotations, nine out of ten people would never look a gift horse in the mouth. Please believe there has been no coercion, but I know what is best for each 'life' in all scenarios, throughout every dimension.

Upon the 'earth-plane' at this time, much conflict and heartache persist. Mother Nature is often frustrated with floods, fires, and many other means by which to express her 'being'. Through all these situations and experiences or tests, humankind endures and can become strengthened, with many shining brighter than ever before. Like a patchwork quilt or blanket, you are each a segment, connecting and playing out their part to expand the consciousness of love and light.

Therefore, to summarize this lesson: your souls are like comets and asteroids which collected small or large pieces of dirt and debris, becoming darker with every new bodily overcoat that's worn. I promise to steer you away from these never-ending cycles, where perceived mistakes are repeated.

My love will guide you through the restless atmosphere of many eras, so you may become shooting stars, burning away karmic dust and grime to reveal your eternal brightness of a thousand or billion suns. As such, the permanent bliss of peace awaits you, always and forever within my heart. Amen."

The sweet sound of the bell chimed. With notepad and pen in hand, the meditation had started. It was as if Baba was already here, waiting. "Welcome! I bring you colours of life, and the energy they create shall infiltrate your beings. May a rainbow shine through your hearts to lift your love to greater heights … and spread further than you ever thought possible. My love, your love, one love is eternal."

Keith: Orange–"My robe encompasses thee … we are one. Comprehend that I protect and guide you. Understand I know what you need and require … please trust in me. God's love flows from, through and to you. Let it uplift other hearts so they experience and learn to do the same."

Kimmy: Purple–"The energy I send pierces the doubt that can rear its ugly head. Always be true and be you. The strength shall be given to maintain faith and one's conviction … if and when the path you tread seems lonely or fraught with concern. God's love is the light which will always guide your true path."

Kate: Green– "The energy of nature surrounds you dear child, and I am highlighting this fact for you to connect with those more subtle of vibrations in the ether. Trees, flowers, birds … and insects all resonate with the same life force that empowers your body. By nurturing nature you expand the same 'force' and power that flows through Creation. God's love shines in the tiniest or greatest of animals or beings. May your own light become an even greater beacon for those who struggle to recognise it within or around themselves."

Robert: Golden yellow–"The energy of the Sun/Son vibrates to and through from head and heart and soul. It illuminates in every direction.

It pierces and cleanses and brings light to even the darkest of places. Whether awake or asleep, may the work you do upon the different levels of time and dimension have an even greater purpose. Reasons for one's endeavours are not always recognisable to you, but they are to me. Continue to work and expand beyond the limits of the mind."

To the circle and all those present in spirit, "Laughter and joy heal many ill's! I am always present, remember. Peace."

Circle:

"Lokah Samastah Sukhino Bhavantu,
Lokah Samastah Sukhino Bhavantu,
Lokah Samastah Sukhino Bhavantu

Shanti, Shanti, Shanti!"

That was incredible! What a lovely atmosphere/energy in tonight's meeting. We all feel eternally blessed. After closing prayers and healing—and our most humble thanks to Swami—messages from the meditation experiences and the transcribed guidance were shared holding the feather. After partaking Vibhuti, Robert and Kate served up some sweet treats. We relaxed and chatted over a welcome cup of tea ... before my journey home. Thank you again, dear Swam! Om Sai Ram/Amen.

In one Circle during a very cold winter, it was brilliant to receive Swami's messages linked to flowers. They are so uplifting and encouraging and colourful ... full of beautiful and brilliant guidance to help us all. Sai constantly motivates and encourages and reminds us of our true nature, and how to conduct ourselves while on this earth plane/physical sojourn.

We caught up with each other's news and got ourselves ready for the evening. Robert addressed the group and said an opening prayer too, followed by the mantra:

> *"Aum Bhur Bhurvah Suvah*
> *Tat Savitur Varenyam*
> *Bhargo Devasya Dheemahi*
> *Dhiyo yonah Prachodayat."*

I then read the following lesson: **WINTER**

"As the wind outside howls around your windows and doors, I welcome you to feel the warmth and sustenance 'within'. Here, you will find peace, contentment, and the answers you seek.

For many, the approach of the year-end is fast and furious ... just like the gales, which seem to throw you off balance as you walk through your journey called life. Similarly, there are those who believe what they are going through has culminated into a 'winter of discontent', with fear and anguish prominent in both hearts and minds.

Will I still be at work in 6-or 12-months' time? How can I find the money for Christmas? What will the future hold for me? Surely, next year must be better?' Well, no wonder illness, stress, and disease continually escalate and surface from those unknown depths of one's own shadow of illusion and confusion.

I appreciate how someone with good health, or without financial or family concerns can state, Just get on with it' or to say one must simply, 'Rise above their so-called problems and fears'. In contrast, others may wish to offer guidance and support to those who 'suffer' and state, "I can understand what you are going through". However, unless one experiences the same conditions resulting in identical outcomes, this is untrue.

Of course, as pleasing as it is to empathize, sympathize and try to impart wisdom, a far greater importance for those who imagine they are entrapped by 'winter blues', anxiety, and trepidation, is to receive your love ... which shines from your heart. Therefore, one must accept the mind, through its own weakness, will occasionally attempt to inflict burdens upon a soul.

If left unchecked or isolated by so-called friends or loved ones, this makes the person feel stripped bare and exposed ... like a tree, devoid of leaves or bark.

Please comprehend, any being or element of life—without the wisdom of who, what, or why they exist—can become more vulnerable. They believe they are separated or alone, and in trying to weather their own storm of emotions, may reach a breaking point.

Mentally, they can snap. Impulses of the mind's 'consciousness' to the brain shear off. These resemble twigs, then large branches, which break under the pressure, falling away to hit the ground. Left unattended, the body suffers the most. Over time, this can be prolonged ... by the denial of self, or by being cast aside, ignored by the bonds and ties of either blood or water. Eventually, they can crack because of the unbearable strain, sensing only one way out, succumbing to self-neglect or instigating a moment of no return.

As one reads—or hears—this, many I's (and eyes) may view these words in a different light. They become illuminated by what they must achieve, or at least start attempting to integrate truth into one's life. Others will have a slower inkling of what direction they are headed, but even though all paths are each your own, you are never alone, as I keep reiterating to every one of you.

People often assume they are taking part in a worthless job. Or, by working in dirty or difficult conditions, they are less important than those who appear to be at the top of the 'tree'—but this makes no difference to me. You must therefore appreciate your own self-worth, because as souls and hearts of love, you are all precious beyond compare. I love you. So, please realise those imagined obstacles and tasks to overcome actually help you develop your character, personality, and should strengthen you, too.

During one's life, if you cannot open your heart and talk to someone else, become 'still'. You can confide in me; in the knowledge I shall not turn you away. I know you better than you can ever know yourself, and am never ashamed of whom, what and why you 'are'. I understand you and will help and guide you, as I love you for all eternity.

Forever your friend and confidant, I am your rock to cling to when all else seems lost around you. I am the light within the darkness, and the helping hand to lift you off the ground when you fall to your knees. I will quench your thirst for knowledge and lead you to the wisdom you need There is always an answer; a way out of the debris and fallout when the emotional storm appears to engulf you in your life.

Appreciate that in all religions and faiths, I am one God. I am love. Nowhere is it written you should hurt or kill. Throughout the eons of time, so many souls believe in their own division from me, igniting karmic imbalance, fuelling desire and inhumane qualities.

They resemble dry autumn leaves burning in a woodland fire. These cause rising embers to fly into the air and ether, effectively landing in distant places, spreading like a plague of ill thoughts and deeds towards other hearts.

So, it is imperative to elevate oneself above anxiety and fear, as negativity can spiral out of control. Realise too, in the far reaches and depths of one's own despair lies a monster called depression. Being aware of these offers a chink of light. This enables you to hang onto truth and hope and be ready to fight your own inner demons of self-doubt and self-worth.

For those close by, sometimes the signs of this appear invisible, even to a best friend, husband, wife, partner, or lover. The tracks and traces often disappear, like footprints in the snow, being erased and covered over by a fresh flurry from above. Throughout your life, it is vital you discover both strength and inspiration. No matter how or where you find them (as long as it is through truth), those dark clouds will fade, turbulent times and situations will ease—which calm you down—and new light will guide you. No longer shall you walk in your own shadow, as this will become a distant memory behind you.

So, how are you now? Well, only you can answer this, but what is important is that you can find your own truth and joy inside you. Whatever thoughts are emanating deep within your heart, they act like a mirror, reflecting way beyond the world in which you live.

In fact, everything is cause and effect., and one can attract so much positive energy by being so. Conversely, negativity combines both fear and dread. Do not misinterpret fate with hate, or life as only light, because one has to bear and love all seasons, all colours of man and the so-called 'good and bad' times with equanimity, too. If

I am in you, I am in all things. If you accept this, then surely your acceptance of each other can be the same.

Remember, the sun—and Son—will always rise somewhere upon the Earth. Love always rises to the surface of your heart when you let your smile, handshake, and every thought and word and deed be the reflection from oneself to simply 'self'. Try then to believe the chill of negative times is a mirage. May each day bring a warm glow to radiate through your kindness and laughter forever and a day. In doing so, you will discover your true power, and therefore find me. Amen."

After the reading, I calmed my breathing rate ready for the meditation. The bell was rung. Pen in hand, I sat still in the hope that Sai would bless us with His presence and grace once more. A few moments passed and in my mind's eye a figure started to appear in the centre of the room. Baba was here! "Welcome my dear children of light. I bring my essence, my bliss to you and all those who gather far beyond these four walls. You are my devotees and I am devoted to you, one and all. May the petals of my heart fall upon your own. Allow the fragrance of our divinity permeate your souls. Perfume, sweet and pure will radiate from and through and to you always in truth and love."

Keith: "Lavender ... butterflies and bees are drawn to it. May the sense of truth illuminate through your heart, for it attracts those in need of your support and guidance. Remember, you are free to share the love within. Know it has no bounds. It is endless, like the connection between us."

Kimmy: "Orange blossom ... the colour orange symbolises my earthly appearance, but like the blossom cast across the wind, my essence is everywhere and resides in everything. In time the fruit is reborn, just like your energy and power and faith it contains it continues in all forms throughout creation may your love and healing be carried to where it needs to be."

Kate: "Sunflowers ... courage grow steadfastly upwards and become an example for all to see. You have an untapped inner strength so believe it to be true and your path will become clearer. Be the true you. Shine and bloom as you face the sun. Then when self-realization takes place, you will be the example that stands tall for all to see."

Julie: " A pink Rose ... my love, your love and our love. Understand when the petals eventually fall they resemble a tear of truth. Anytime these well up inside the heart know they are pure and unsullied by fear or pain or anger or doubt. Remember the well can never run dry for I am the totality of emotions which flows from soul to soul and heart to heart."

Robert: "Lemongrass ... yellow with the scent of citrus. I am the freshness that brings in the new, into every aspect of your life. Understand I am the radiance that shines eternal and allow the light to permeate in everything you say and think and do. I am near so never fear, remember!"

Once again Baba then stayed in the centre of the room. Silent. Before he departed, his wonderful smile radiated love and purity and truth. He raised His right hand and as quickly as he had arrived ... he was gone. The meditation had concluded and as always, precisely on time as the bell was chimed.

All the circle awake from their stillness. We sent absent healing and ended with prayers and salutations to Swami. Circle:

> *"Lokah Samastah Sukhino Bhavantu,*
> *Lokah Samastah Sukhino Bhavantu,*
> *Lokah Samastah Sukhino Bhavantu*
>
> *Shanti, Shanti, Shanti!"*

After we had a cup of tea and snacks, I held the white feather and gratefully share Sai's messages to each of the group. A few of the devotees shared some messages, too. We are truly humbled and eternally grateful by what has been given to us all. Thanks be to God! Om Sai Ram/Amen.

CHRISTMAS AND SPIRITUAL 'GIFTS'

I always looked forward to seeing everyone in the group, though especially in the run up to Christmas. We were often blessed ... to not only bear witness to Sai's presence, but sometimes Lord Jesus too! These occasions, where both 'light bodies' could be visualized, were incredible indeed.

Such joy would fill our hearts, and one could sense tremendous energy within the room. It felt immensely powerful and peaceful. It was as if their love flowed through us. Robert opened the meeting with a prayer an salutations to Baba before we all chanted the mantra. Circle:

> *"Aum Bhur Bhurvah Suvah*
> *Tat Savitur Varenyam*
> *Bhargo Devasya Dheemahi*
> *Dhiyo yonah Prachodayat."*

Lesson: **STAR of WONDER**

"Welcome once more to one and all, but deep inside the heart, can you really hear my call? For I am here, there, and am everywhere ... even beside you in the next chair ... and always within and never without, so why do you wish to scream and shout?

Do not believe in false riddles or jokes, during the time for high spirits, so be careful not to choke. And as Christmas arrives at your home and your heart, why do many souls now cry and fall apart?

With so much stress and cause for '*dis*-ease', as one-half stands and others bend knees. Though forgiveness and joy do the many now wish, others look blank as they cross off their list. They ask shall I give, or will I receive, when the truth reveals ... 'you all get what you need'.

The hungry and the poor simply cry out in vain, as those who walk by, sometimes glance of disdain. So, who is the happier as both expressions had met ... the rich in the wallet or within heart instead?

Do you shine as the 'hustle' and the 'bustle' pick up pace, with cards to write, and oh so many calls to now make? Can you radiate and glisten as the 25th draws near, or does the eve and the day, bring out dread and new fears?

For you all have a decision, to glow like the 'Son', each day and by night, until your victory is won. So please try wearing smiles, with new selfless frowns, or do you take party frocks and trade them all in for nightgowns?

However, to hide light away so that no one can see, just disguises the real you, and of course the real me. For a wardrobe so deep, displays the true choice, as garments masquerade, like a change in your voice. Indeed, you can even dress up, in whatever one likes, but the truth of it all, the world grips like a vice.

Therefore, who holds you in place; for it must only be self, contained in four walls, not by goblins or elves. So, I urge you to walk, and find new chinks of light, the way out and way in, as its love at first sight.

For you can discover, a new freedom and expression, as open hands lay before ... you will realise the score. The eternal goal you must reach, in unison and as one, for all can move on to live and become.

With the pathway I set, countless eons ago, laid out before you, as your heart will now know. With many people and new friends, to come into your life, some will stay single, or take husbands or wives.

All are entwined as fragments of me, and everyone is linked and must return to the tree. Like branches and twigs, you reach out near and far, as relatives and kin, travel through time, not by car.

Throughout creation and the universe, love reigns supreme ... opened hearts and minds know of just what I mean. Please trust within me, to search and discover, what lies in the distance, but not undercover.

With galaxies and constellations, too many to mention, simply expand your horizon ... isn't that your intention? For the stars and the planets, they all mesmerise, but the truth is inside, and not seen with your eyes.

It is beautiful and magnificent, no earthly words could describe ... glittering prize to behold, and only beyond mind. For thoughts often trick you, into thinking what is best, forget false desire, as love does the rest.

So, while looking at the sky, upon dark starry nights, what do you wish for or fear, go to ground or take flight? Is your head in the clouds, as some state you are, or is your heart far above, so-called madness of crowd?

One should be who you are, and what you were born unto be ... an expression of love, made of you and of me. Do not pass into shade, of past duties or time, rather walk to the glory, of the light so divine.

For every moment or step, which you take towards me; the closer I become, for I shall take three. Sincerely I wish, for your good conduct in life ... no ultimatum or test but living in love is the best.

My grace is abundant, and is forever please trust, so having faith within me, and inside, is a must. So, rise above times, when you cry or breakdown, for I will protect you forever, with light from my crown.

When my 'glory' shines down, some hearts may not feel, if you then turn away, from friends and family who are real. By linking arms and your hands, with neighbours as one, the world can still change, and it has already begun.

This is hard to be seen, and for you to realise when violence and hatred seem forever to rise. Therefore, do not succumb, to what the media or politics portray, but do all that you can, to help lead man from decay.

With everyday choices and these are your own; try leading by example, and not by false throne. Act then in truth, to achieve the extra mile, for always I am with you ... whether meek or the mild.

No matter if an adult, even teenager or child, what is your dream, and what makes you smile? And if I made ... your one wish come true, what would you ask me, and is it for you?

More money, a job, new clothes, or new life, perhaps a change of your body, but not by a knife? Do not become down, by any trouble and strife, or think you are unloved, because that is not right.

Because you are everything and in truth come from me, not separate, or divided, for that could not be. Indeed, your essence and your beauty cannot be called into question, no matter what debate or arguments are mentioned.

For you and I both know, this all to be true, simply put we are 'one,' so do not feel shame or be blue. This Christmas time, then, please forgive and forget ... the pain or the anguish, by which karma may have set.

Instead, please be joyful and reach out from your heart, as true love is eternal, and there from the start. As in the past and the present, it's time to decorate your home, live to the full and in peace ... beyond speech or the phone.

For the star of wonder, you now place upon the tree, represents a 'life' beyond dreams, and is your true reality! Happy Christmas to you all. Amen."

We settled down and the group mentioned how lovely, and poignant, the reading had been. The subtle chime of the bell somehow seemed to resonate longer this evening. The meditation started, and I reflected upon the quietness and stillness that soon enveloped us all. Suddenly Baba arrived ... wearing his usual bright orange robe/gown. As I gazed upon him, it suddenly changed to brilliant white. This reminded me of his celebration/ceremony attire.

Almost immediately, Jesus appeared by his right hand–all in white too–as if they illuminated each other. They stood side by side, surveying the room. Above their heads, translucent clouds formed, then elegantly swirled in a clockwise direction. I could make out the shapes of many Angels hovering within them. Their wings seemed to expand and interlink above the circle, and I knew this was for protection and keeping any negativity at bay.

Jesus 'floated' towards us. In turn, he placed a beautiful rose (and a separate thorn), in each of our right hands. I gathered they represented both joy and light, and the contrasting pain and darkness, that can appear in every life ... at any time.

I am seeing a manger appear in the centre of the room. The three wise men are bearing gifts ... they are presents for us in the 'present' moment. Swami is happy and smiling.

Issy, on my left, is deep in meditation. Jesus kneels before her, for the Lord kneels to the same divinity of each 'therein'. A small ornate purple box, wrapped with golden braid (a ribbon with a bow) is placed in her hands. "The bow represents an unbroken connection to God and for enlightenment. It is ready to be opened now, and the energy contained within is to be utilised."

Keith is presented with a gem, a green emerald. A link to Ireland came into my mind. "The Lord will polish and refine you into peace and bliss."

Kimmy held an orange. Amber seemed prevalent as a preservative. "You must persevere ... hold fast to the truth to overcome all doubt and doubters. Remember, eternal light is not man-made. Please keep your heart always open."

Kate was holding her special rose. I gazed intently and observed its crimson colour. "As God's child understand your bloodline. The spark of your divinity is energy and purity. Like a fire cleansing phoenix from the ashes ... to rise in my glory."

Julie's hands were wide from her body as if holding something else ... as if she embraced an ocean vista. Blue waves seemed to gently pass through her fingers. "You are my wave and we merge into 'one'. Go with the flow. Know that the tide will turn in your favour. Don't feel 'blue' as life is to be lived in joy ... my joy ... eternal Joy."

Robert seemed very peaceful. A violet colour descended over him. "I give you Indigo ... for inwards you go to help you unveil the radiance and spark of life." (It is like a neon light and reflective). "Understand the exterior is only a reflection of the interior so I urge you to reflect upon these words to radiate peace and goodwill."

I gaze around the room once more before Sai seems to expand and touch each of our bodies. Threads from his gown appear to unravel and he spoke, "Know that these threads from my gown connect you all into eternity. So, be at peace, especially at his festive time."

Within a few seconds, the vibrant glow of their divinity began to dissipate. The outline of their 'bodies' began to fade as Robert's meditation bell was rung … signalling the end of the 30 minutes. Wow! What blessings have been bestowed upon us all!

We gave absent healing and prayers, then closed the circle:

> *"Lokah Samastah Sukhino Bhavantu,*
> *Lokah Samastah Sukhino Bhavantu,*
> *Lokah Samastah Sukhino Bhavantu*
>
> *Shanti, Shanti, Shanti!"*

After sharing Vibhuti, I held the feather last of all, and read Swami's guidance with the group. Robert and Kate then made the drinks. They had earlier prepared some lovely food on their dining room table, which we were all extremely grateful for. I guess you could say it was our physical sustenance to go along with the spiritual sustenance we had been blessed to receive from Sai! Another wonderful meeting indeed. My drive home was full of thoughts and gratitude for all the love and light our special Circle receives. Thank you once again, dear Heavenly Father/Mother God! Om Sai Ram … Amen.

The following Circle/meeting contained fabulous guidance, and a lot of this revolved around gifts ... spiritual Christmas 'presents' that we humbly and gratefully received!

It was lovely to meet up again with the group. We discussed how things were with each of us, any important news to share ... any spiritual experiences that had occurred in our lives since we last met. There was time for a quick drink before Robert gave an opening prayer. We paused for moment to become still, then chanted the Gayatri Mantra as always, which always resonates through me.

> *"Aum Bhur Bhurvah Suvah*
> *Tat Savitur Varenyam*
> *Bhargo Devasya Dheemahi*
> *Dhiyo yonah Prachodayat."*

I then read the following lesson: **THREE**

"Within the silence, thoughts and feelings now emerge, but are these from the mind, the heart or from both? Perhaps our love transmutes, and then releases these from your soul? Well, today I will explain and let you digest what I mean regarding these things, as many people who read and contemplate upon this will discover a greater understanding of what is involved, and the process by which they need to strive and pursue to reach their true goal.

Therefore, someone thinking of the word 'three' may initially think of the numerical number or perhaps engage in a deeper expanding thought. This could range from simple numerology or by considering the power encompassing mind, body, and spirit; the Father, Son and Holy Ghost ... and even faith, hope and charity. Someone may express or describe each of these elements as the Holy Trinity, but please put any preconceptions to one side. In order to simplify life, one must try to understand ... man, beast, and God.

During the rituals of working, eating, and sleeping, as well as those thoughts, words, and deeds you subconsciously and consciously engage in ... all contain both choices and decisions to make, and each takes one of the aforementioned forms. In fact, not only one but also all three can control your desires, hopes, and dreams.

If you kindly help another living thing, do you realise what has actually taken place? When hurtful actions, words, or thoughts have manifested themselves far beyond your four walls, are they human, godly, or of a beastly trait? Regarding your daily situations, try to place what they imprint on the mind and contemplate the direct result and outcome of such things ... or simply let the 'impression' of the information drip through to your consciousness and fall upon your heart.

In addition, consider whether the feelings and thoughts of 'desire'—whether they are material, mental or physical—are degrading the resulting actions you take? Does the need or dependency (in its various forms) envelope and make you feel different in any way? When you analyse these, do they reveal any lowering in the vibration and energy of your soul?

Some say they do, as one can become animalistic, 'beastly' and even 'ungodly'. Therefore, if you choose the resulting consequence of all your actions, thoughts, and deeds, then one must strive for only one eventuality, and this should be 'godly'. Is this easier said than done ... of course it is!

The inquirer, the aspirant, or the devotee must always consider the outcome, and in doing so, which of the 'three' will prevail. In reality, for every soul to reach the goal of eternal bliss in me, then a divine result must be the number one priority ... the winner, and the master of all things. Do not waver or doubt your success. If you were to think of such as a race, some will give up. Others get side-tracked, taking what they believe are smoother roads when none exist.

How long does this take? Well, did the tortoise not beat the hare in the tale and fable? For instance, you may find the path you take is short, but for some, it means their whole lifetime. Remember, do not class your own road and journey above another's, because each of you live with your own karma to balance and work through. So do not judge; lest ye be judged.

Try to eliminate any concerns over 'time', in terms of your days, weeks, months or years, as it waits for no man, and you cannot alter this. Comprehend I am the shoreline and your harbour instead, for within me—and you—are where you will find eternal rest and peace.

Understand too, as each morning breaks, and the Sun rises in the phenomenal world, the light brings warmth and substance to all living things. In the same way, the illumination of your heart and soul radiates and reflects all you are, have been, and will be. Your whole being can reveal these as human, beast, or godly actions and qualities.

This is important, because as you grow and mature, these 'three' elements become expressed through your character, personality, and attitudes, and in fact, with everyone you meet too. Indeed, every environment or situation will cause you to think and react in the way described.

Only by experiencing the truth of your search (during daily life), dictates the outcome. Remember, your divinity holds no doubts, and shares no blame or shame, and while the outer casing (which is your body) conceals the beauty and peace, it still allows the illusion and confusion to rain through, too. Therein lies the choice … from deep inside you.

Please appreciate, at Christmas, people seem to despise, want, or need something, which is usually in the material sense. For example, picture a child ripping open a present, fervently casting aside the wrapping paper in their eagerness to see the 'prize' inside. Through their enthusiasm to reveal and know what it contains, they take no time to see who sent it, and some parents (or next of kin) may become annoyed or even anguished by this, citing their child's sheer excitement got the better of them. Everyone should have this same desperation and yearning, but for the gift of love, light, and truth instead ... and I too wish you all to experience the joy, unveiling what you so desperately seek and need.

In reality, the outer 'wrapping' (over the true you), is impermanent, and is therefore cast aside to be buried or burnt. Well, I am not concerned with everything that envelopes your divinity within, for your looks, appearance, and material wealth are all by-products and unsustainable.

On one's rebirth and embodiment, you possess nothing of the material world you enter, and so you return 'without' too. Only the essence and growth of your soul and being remain intact, and your karma will have played its part in balancing, erasing, or even multiplying this.

In the earlier example, the child did not wait to see who gave them their gift, whereas true love—which is you—cannot be labelled. No tag is required in order to express a 'to' and 'from' … because love is, was, and always will be. Indeed, love is in all creation and both you and me. It is this, above all things, that makes you 'godly', and because of this; is the element of the 'three' that will live forevermore. Therefore, in peace and blessings live your today, for you are my gift and the present—I have pre-sent—for we are all one. Amen."

I did some breath work, whereby I slowed my breathing rate down ... inhaling and exhaling softly before the meditation began. Pen and notepad to hand, I was eager to write down what was about to take place.

A fine mist, like silver stardust, descended in the air and started to form a circle above our heads. Spiritual energy spun in a clockwise direction which resembled a glorious crown of light. After a few seconds, whispers of ethereal light appeared like spokes form the centre of a wheel. These were tethers attached to our hearts and minds and souls. Unity and peace was our connection to Swami.

Baba appeared, "I'm here. Happy, together ... oneness. A family of light ... all children of my heart." Sai waved His right hand and items immediately float through the ether towards each of us.

Issy: A blue book landed on her lap. I realised it was a bible, with gold lettering and a small crucifix on the front. There was a reference to John1:16. The horizontal bar (symbolic of the ego) cuts across the vertical 'I'. Sai speaks, "The legacy of love and the end of ego has past. Now soar high like an eagle." (**John 1:16 ... And of His fullness we have all received and grace for grace.** NB: Indicating that Christ the Word is the source of grace. Grace is all that God is free to do for us based on the work of Christ. In this verse the apostle reminds his readers that they have already experienced grace in abundant measure. The word **And** refers to verse 14 where beholding the glory of Christ was stated. In addition, the word **'fullness'** complete adequacy of God's nature in Christ. The wonder of the Son stepping into a human body with grace is a fullness never before seen prior to the incarnation. Christ is abundant in the blessings He offers. He gives and we receive).

Robert: A white feather spirals floating up and down and back and forth in front of him, accompanied with soft, musical notes. It moved like a conductor in front of an orchestra. "Now orchestrate, be a master of your own energy. Travers the high and low notes–like life's experiences with equanimity."

Keith: A button, as if a replacement for one on a jacket? "This is for the overcoat of the soul ... your body. It will provide you with the extra versatility and protection from the elements and elemental energies of fire, water, air and earth ... bringing balance to you."

Kimmy: A pair of shoes appears out of thin air and she's suddenly wearing them! "With these comes a new path to tread, along with the ability to do so with the purpose, comfort and ease and protection. The energy they bring grounds you–temporarily–so that your love can work on a different level ... to support and help those in need at this time, those who need guiding towards the light."

Kate: An umbrella swirls down and she holds the handle tightly. "This provides protection for and against the elements. In addition, to shield the mental aspect of your being. The mind can get misguided, but love and light is stronger than negativity and can bring you peace of mind .. and a restful heart. Know that I watch over you ... as I watch over you all."

Julie: A key descends and enters her heart. "Your love is both the key and the lock. People often believe they have one or the other, and keep searching for a mysterious door that leads to me. Why search when I am you and you are me ... remember? You already have everything you could ever need or want. You just need to think it, imagine it, believe it and it will come true."

I look upwards, and see a large olive branch that stretches across the ceiling. Leaves start falling around the room, then form lines towards Swami ... like a magnet drawing iron filings. "I am forever here for you all. Follow the trail, though some may say it's a trial. Understand, all you have to do is reach for me, call me, just think of me, and then realise I am already there ... within and without, above and below you. We are 'one' for all eternity." Swami raises his hand and drifts out of my view.

The meditation is over as the chime of the bell resonates and breaks the silence. We all send out absent healing. and prayers and salutations, too. Robert then provides Vibhuti for us all. Circle:

"Lokah Samastah Sukhino Bhavantu,
Lokah Samastah Sukhino Bhavantu,
Lokah Samastah Sukhino Bhavantu

Shanti, Shanti, Shanti!"

What an awesome experience ... very moving indeed. When it was my turn for holding the white feather, I shared the messages with everyone and these were humbly accepted. I still can't believe how fortunate we all are to receive His presence and blessings and grace and presents. too!. Thank you beloved Baba. Om Sai Ram/Amen.

During another Christmas gathering one year, Swami provided us with further wonderful symbolism. A joyous festive occasion indeed. After greetings, and prayers we settled for the evening. We chanted the Mantra, followed by a reading. Circle:

> *"Aum Bhur Bhurvah Suvah*
> *Tat Savitur Varenyam*
> *Bhargo Devasya Dheemahi*
> *Dhiyo yonah Prachodayat."*

Lesson: **DIAMONDS**

"I welcome you all to the last lesson of the year, but by no means is it the end of love, light, and truth. Even though there are now many lessons to draw upon, many souls wish for further help and advice in the form of the written word. The where and the when, of course, will become known in good time, and for the 'pen' to communicate spiritual guidance, education, and wisdom from, through, and to the heart once more.

So, as each lesson becomes etched in your mind and relayed deep within you, what prevents these words from disappearing into the ether or fading from memory? Surely, such messages being conveyed with ink can only lighten and grow fainter over time?

Well, the truth is different. This is being written with permanence, like a diamond upon granite. You see, for something to be real and tangible, and become pure inside you, unless it resonates with simplicity, it would be like chalk on pavements, washed away by the emotional tears which rain down from thy heart. Similarly, with text, when written into the sands of time, it can be easily erased by the winds of change.

Please appreciate love flows like light. It can travel through a diamond, unhindered by the denseness of the world in which you live.

In fact, this is a prized jewel. Its unique qualities make it a valuable and true 'currency' where your physical resides.

Likewise, every human being and soul are precious. And beyond priceless. You are each a living flame and an expression of me, forming the crown of my heart. Indeed, you are all the embodiment of my love. As divinity personified, billions of you—and every being too—cannot say one is worth more than another, or indeed greater than anything else.

In reality, whether rich, poor, meek, or mild; and if one is white, yellow, red, or black, you just have different facets, shapes, sizes, characters, and personalities which make you unique. Your karma may reflect your imperfections, those chips, dents, and scratches caused only by—and to—each other. A diamond can only affect another, and vice versa, remember.

Your own thoughts, words, and deeds make all limitations. No intervening hand creates them to inflict pain or hardship, or by making some feel less worthy, unloved, or alone. No, only truth is highlighted and revealed as waves and beams of light. Someone cannot manipulate or disguise these, like throwing a wet blanket over flames, snuffing out a candle, or by flicking a switch to off.

Comprehend the term 'do not fear when I am near', because love always finds a way through the shadows of illusion and confusion. Likewise, we both have the same goal, which is to smooth out and erase any exterior imperfections of hate, anger, jealousy, and ego. Your inner search for peace, bliss, and self-realization then becomes much easier to materialize and achieve.

One may sometimes think that this—or I—am hard to find, but how often would you find a precious jewel just sitting there on the ground? Please understand, by turning within to the stillness and peace, you are digging below the surface, searching towards the light at the end of the tunnel. With perseverance, stamina, and determination—combined with positive thoughts and words and deeds—I guarantee you will succeed. Everything worth having is more satisfying if attained this way, is it not? Remember, I am with you. If you trust in me, letting me work through you … then you cannot fail.

In terms of divinity, I am the expression of love, for no soul was ever born with a silver spoon in its mouth. In fact, firstly you were never born at all, but were already part of me. Second, every single spark of light has developed themselves through experience and knowledge, bringing wisdom from deep within.

Like film inside an old camera, one can stay seemingly—and falsely—contained in its casement … called the 'body'. The flash—light—of the mind only illuminates the truth when it is ready to, which deceives many into thinking the world is full of shadow and doubt when it is not. Therefore, the negativity needs to be transformed through this pretend and so-called darkened room of—and upon—Earth to reveal the picture of truth.

Once exposed, the mind, heart, and soul—in unison—can bear witness to the glory of our love. The pieces of one's life—like a jigsaw puzzle discussed once before—shall come together. Then you can then frame this (to be displayed) for all to view who, what, and why you truly are divine.

Some of you take time to develop, like the images of 'old'. Others may resemble and be like a digital camera, revealing an image or scene almost instantaneously to be viewed by one's 'self', or by another. Imagine if a photograph were taken of you right now, how would that make you feel? Is your hair, okay? Do you think you ought to change how you dress and look? What sort of makeover do you think would make you happy, and more content? And if so, who are you then trying to please? Is it the photographer, perhaps your friends or family, even strangers ... or is it for yourself?

Everything comes from within, but your face becomes a canvass, displaying and radiating love or hate ... as your smile or frown can elevate or cause a debate. Know that while technology can disguise and manipulate those tracks of your tears from red eyes ... they cannot be hidden from me. Therefore, I understand and know you, and moreover, of what you need, when you need it, and why.

I hope you try to be yourself, and happy in your own skin. Through thick and thin, hold on to your own beliefs and faith if they are true. Be able to look in the mirror, accept, and like what you see. Let everything you say, think and do be the real reflection of your own heart ... and not what someone else thinks what they wish to see, or for you to be.

In all relationships, there is give and take. There may be compromise and forgiveness, gratitude and understanding, but that gives no other person the right to treat another as a doormat, by leaving their unwanted feelings or traits at someone else's door.

Okay, it is now time to close once more, but I ask every soul and spark of divinity to shine and reflect their love towards, and through, and from each other. Be polished in all that's said and done ... not covered by dust, dirt, or debris, falsely disguised by the impermanent world around you.

I love you. I believe in you. If I could desire or perhaps wish anything for you all, it would be for you to recognize and become your own love ... which eternally abides and lives in every heart and soul. Amen."

After this reading I did some breathe work for a couple of minutes while the group refocused, ready for the meditation. The table bell was rung, and the thirty minutes silence had begun.

Baba soon appeared, slowly walking around the circle ... hands behind His back. He paused in front of the fireplace as usual and his physical shape seemed to change in to a brilliant star ... a beacon of joy and peace. "Gather around dear children of light. The love of the Lord is within and upon thee. Each soul will grow and know the truth 'of and from and through' the light." After a few seconds, Swami's face and crown of hair became noticeable once more as the glow and illumination of the star diminished. " I bring you gifts from Heaven, within the Lord's care."

I turned my gaze towards Robert. A scarlet coloured box, adorned with beautiful gold ribbon was placed in his hands. Magically, it unwrapped itself to reveal an amazing camera lens, "You will have new focus, the ability to see and comprehend 'life' in greater detail. The lens of the physical, your third eye and the heart provides spiritual insight to be utilised in conjunction with each other."

(Rob is a very good photographer and has many beautiful photos in his collection).

Keith: An oblong shaped, emerald coloured parcel with a silver ribbon sat in Keith's lap. It opened and a musical scroll sat inside. The notes upon it started to play. It was the song entitled <u>'Needles and Pins'</u> sang by the Searchers. (Written by Sonny Bono and Jack Nitzche). I could hear verse three:

> 'I saw her today, I saw her face
> It was a face I loved, and I knew,
> I had to run away…
> And get down on my knees and pray,
> That they'd go away'

"These notes and feelings are like the highs and lows of life. A reminder and the support to aid your concentration because you control your destiny through thought. This allows for good vibrations and energy to manifest."

Kimmy: A ball wrapped in gold paper laid in her hands. "This represents the Sun and Son inside ... for each soul is eternal. The physical body is only an expression of me, but in reality it is false, a wrapping which mirrors the truth within. This gift, therefore, is a reminder of life over death."

Kate: Her present is already unwrapped, it's a small pyramid ... multi-coloured on each side/face. "Like a pyramid, a strong base and foundations are provided to which you can strive and continue forwards, onwards, and upwards. This gift will point you in the right direction. Most people want to reach for the stars, but now you are aware that you already exist beyond the beyond ... because the love you are, cannot be erased or diminished."

Suddenly, I started to hear chimes of many bells resembling almost silent echoes across time and space (and yet ringing out) to attract all life to see, heal, touch, feel and know ... love. Then, the elevation of angelic voices, joyfully singing Christmas carols ... in praise to God.

'Star of Wonder, Star of Light, Star of Royal Beauty Bright...'

I felt cocooned within a state of bliss, as Sai's face and that of Jesus seemed to merge into 'one'. "Know that I watch over you all. Keep strong and positive in all you do."

The meditation ended, and we followed with our prayers and salutations. Robert then shared Vibhuti with us. Circle:

CHRISTMAS AND SPIRITUAL 'GIFTS'

"Lokah Samastah Sukhino Bhavantu,
Lokah Samastah Sukhino Bhavantu,
Lokah Samastah Sukhino Bhavantu

Shanti, Shanti, Shanti!"

I felt most eager when the white feather was passed to me, enabling me to share each person's message and gifts with them. With cups of tea we were treated to some hot mince pies. (You can never have enough mince pies). What an evening! Thank you beloved Baba and dear Lord Jesus ... and to God of all things. Om Sai Ram/ Amen. Circle:

At the end of one year, just 5 days before Christmas, those fortunate to be present were treated to some more amazing gifts from Swami! I'll get straight into the evenings events, and the most brilliant messages that we received!

The room was tremendously peaceful. Robert's and Kate's lounge felt very festive. A small, but wonderful Christmas tree, beautifully decorated, stood in the corner. Fairy lights were strung around the room, which reflected and sparkled in the mirror over the fireplace.

We all had a drink, and then sat ready to become still. However, someone mentioned Christmas carols and there was soon an impromptu rendition of 'Silent Night' which was amazing! After a couple of minutes, everything was quiet once more ... and Robert gave an opening prayer before we chanted the Gayathri Mantra:

"Aum Bhur Bhurvah Suvah
Tat Savitur Varenyam
Bhargo Devasya Dheemahi
Dhiyo yonah Prachodayat."

I then read the Lesson: **HOME**

"I sincerely hope that you not only think about the words on these pages but also sense them in your heart too, because they aim to keep your attention focused and true upon important things in your life.

Now, as Christmas approaches, one's thoughts and feelings undoubtedly turn to family and friends both near and dear at this special time of the year. In addition, regarding your festivities, one cannot but wonder about 'home', and those moments with those who matter most.

Why do you feel this way? Is it tradition, or perhaps your faith? Is one's home where the heart is? Of course, it is natural for someone to conclude this refers to your earthbound dwelling, whether made of wood, tin, brick, or stone. This is likely to contain even the bare minimum of comfort, be it straw for a pillow, cardboard for a bed, pieces of rubbish for a fire, or even the opposite, having luxuries like shelves full of food, a feather mattress, electricity and gas, or shiny televisions and gadgets which attempt to entertain your mind.

Therefore, no matter where and when one thinks of home, memories of sustenance and well-being will come to the fore, which pulls on heartstrings, and makes you wish you were there. And, if you are where you think you ought to be, perhaps someone special, such as a friend, brother, sister, father, mother, lover, partner, husband, or wife, are not.

In this scenario, it is easy to imagine a separation exists between each other, be this through time and space, or even by the veil and curtain which you call death. However, try to remember, above all things, they are actually as close or as distant as you think or believe them to be.

Realise the heart is not just the functioning organ of the body; it is everything, because your heart is mine too, and love unites every soul. Therefore, the connection—when your true desire takes hold—can be as weak or as strong as you make it. Indeed, they say absence makes the heart grow fonder, and if you believe this, take comfort knowing that 'time' may seem so important, but in the grander scheme of things, bears little relevance at all.

Please appreciate, love cannot dissipate and fade like water upon the sand, evaporating in the sun, and therefore the so-called 'separation', even for one minute—or for what transpires to be your whole life—will eventually reveal the truth. You will realise the differences between what is real with the misconceptions the impermanent world tries to impose on you. So, do not gaze towards an empty chair. Instead, hear their voice, see the look in their eyes and smile upon their face. Sense the touch of their hand too in the knowledge they cannot ever be erased, for they are deep inside your heart.

In fact, you may think they have disappeared or somehow drift far away, trying to find a way back to you, but do not feel hurt, sad or grieve, because you must understand, they are not, and never will be lost! I am with every single one of you. I know where each soul resides every second, minute, hour, day, week, month, and year, and for all eternity.

I comprehend so many hearts that ache. They are often torn in two, but just remember, I am like glue … who always returns and binds you all together. I love you, so how can this not be so? I realise one's pain can drive deeper than any blade upon the body, or how words can cut more quickly, and take a lifetime to heal. However, if one can help, share, and speak with truth and love, and another's heart is open and receptive, then it, too, can be given the time and strength to mend.

Know I will be the plaster which is 'cast' towards you by this reality, to repair broken hearts and protect you from the infectious mind and the brittleness of a weakened faith … especially when trials and tribulations seem too much to bear. One day, all souls will appreciate they are on a journey, and each one is different. That said, the destination is the same, and, through self-realization of your own divine essence, you will come to realise your genuine home of bliss and peace.

Within me, your dreams come true. Every day is magical … with love eternally beating from and through and to your heart, and you will recognize this in all its glory. Therefore, by opening the door to your own heart, the Christmas you could only ever imagine becomes reality. Inside is a welcome you will never forget, with cheers and tears of the happy kind, and smiles without fear.

Each room is decorated with pearls of wisdom, and they are all illuminated by both starlight and the 'son'. There is no hate or pain, only truth and fun. There is no empty chair, just two hearts which beat as one. Family, friends and pets, and teachers and guides, all pass through and by, to greet and meet you.

Surely by now, you must accept this gift of love is from no 'secret' Santa, as the glory of you is not meant to be hidden away or pushed aside to pretend it's for another day. No, for every moment is an opportunity to share and sprinkle the glitter of your own divinity.

Sometimes this will rest where you think it should. On other occasions, the words you speak, the gestures you make, and your love will shine and travel to life in the most unlikely of places, throughout time, space, and every dimension. You may not bear witness or understand these results, but that is not important, because every act flowing from your heart transcends and elevates precisely where and when I intended it to. Do not worry or concern yourself over the 'result' of these beautiful actions, for I know the where, what and the how.

So then, with the festivities only a few days away, please reflect upon a new beginning and the rebirth of truth, which has been nurtured deep 'within' yourself. Love has grown inside with all the ingredients installed from my heart to yours … faith, righteousness, non-violence and so much more.

Our connection cannot be severed, and our divinity is my crowning glory for all to witness and partake. Therefore, through infancy, one's youth, in middle or even old age, there is the opportunity to shine through your love, which I have presented and pre-sent to you with all we are—and I am. By opening your heart, all who draw close will recognize the light, and share in something precious to behold, for all eternity. This is my timeless gift to one and all. Amen."

With note pad and pen in hand, and some deep, breath work … I was open and ready to receive what we hoped would be a very special evening of blessings from Baba. The meditation began and Sai immediately appeared.

Swami, "Bless you dear children of light. Many souls gather in the name of love, to partake and share and grow and learn. Whether on the earth-plane, in the ether and levels of vibration … my joy and peace reign. As the end of the year draws near, may you all rejoice in the light from the 'Son'. He guides and directs his flock always and forever, no matter day or night or 'whatever the weather'. Know your hearts flow eternally through His to the mother/father and all life. Be still and receive what is needed for the mind and body and soul at this time."

Keith: "This is my gift ... golden strings for a guitar. My love flows through you dear child, so that you can live by the chords of truth. May the rhythm of your beating heart echo across time and dimensions ... to resonate through those who fear and cannot recognise the light within themselves."

Kimmy: "These woollen gloves/mittens are woven from and through the 'Lamb' of God. They will protect you. They were strengthened the power within, which flows through your hands, those previous healing frequencies that cannot be dissipated."

Kate: "Here is a palette of colour from God. Many different shades and textures can be created through and from your heart. Some remain bright and light, others dark and mysterious. Let your creativity flow, to capture the energy and truth, especially in nature a masterpiece can then be displayed but only because it is a piece of the 'master' which flows through your heart and soul. Remember, everything is one and whole."

Julie: "Your present is a spiritual map. Your work is a reflection of the abilities granted to you. You take a certain route because it enables you to arrive at the correct destination at a certain time. So too your life ... for love guides you to where you are meant to be and when. My help is always there to guide you if necessary, and to swerve and avoid the negativity, which can lead many astray, but not you."

Rob: "I present to you a magnifying glass. This provides additional support when and where required. I will help you to zoom in to understand what is important in this realm and all around you. In addition, this lens will focus your energy at the correct time it is needed to shine. Remember too, in the Sai-lens (silence), you will always experience the truth."

Swami stood in the centre of the circle for a while. Then he appeared to merge with a brilliant light ... an image of Lord Jesus ... a glorious moment and an immense blessing bestowed upon us all. "Merry Christmas. Peace and goodwill to the world. Amen."

The table bell chimed to signal the end of the meditation. The Circle chanted the mantra:

> *"Lokah Samastah Sukhino Bhavantu,*
> *Lokah Samastah Sukhino Bhavantu,*
> *Lokah Samastah Sukhino Bhavantu*
>
> *Shanti, Shanti, Shanti!"*

We gave absent healing and closed with a prayer and further salutations to Baba. The white feather was handed to each other for any guidance to be shared, then I then proceeded to read the spiritual messages and explain the gifts Sai had given to each devotee. Kate served the Christmas treats, including cakes and mince pies with cups of tea. Wow ... what an absolutely incredible Circle it was tonight. Praise be to God in the highest. Om Sai Ram/Amen.

This particular Circle/Sai Baba meditation group, occurred one December in the run up to Christmas. Once again, it was only myself and Kimmy and Keith and Jill present. I had picked Jill up on the way over to Keith's home, and as we pulled up I could see the festive decorations through his lounge window. It always felt extra special to be together, so close to the Lord's birthday!

We had a lovely cup of tea and chatted about all our Christmas plans, where we were each spending the big day, and whether we'd see our family and friends. After about ten minutes we got comfortable and ready for the meditation and spiritual work to come. I lit the candle and incense stick, and we gave an opening prayer for protection and guidance and healing. Chanting the Gayathri Mantra came next:

> *"Aum Bhur Bhurvah Suvah*
> *Tat Savitur Varenyam*
> *Bhargo Devasya Dheemahi*
> *Dhiyo yonah Prachodayat."*

I then read the following lesson, and once again it felt as if it came directly from source/God: **BLESSED**

"One by one, the days of your life continue to roll by. You, as the inquirer, the aspirant or devotee can now pause for thought. Perhaps you'll wonder how far you have come during the past year.

Maybe you'll be considering what life's 'lessons' you have learned, mulling over those decisions and choices you had made within situations of (or over) work, friends and family? You might even recall those actions which caused regret, those so-called mistakes which irritated the mind and heart ... and no amount of wishful thinking can change them.

CHRISTMAS AND SPIRITUAL 'GIFTS'

Yes indeed, every single one of your thoughts, prayers, actions, deeds, and words forms a network of joy or agony. Like the veins within the body—and your spiralling DNA—these are all connected. The results of them all flow like blood to the heart. They either nourish or emanate light, or they carry the sadness of pain and shadow.

As this passage of time (which you call the 'year'), slowly draws to a close ... only a few weeks remain. The Christmas 'period' can begin. Trees will be erected in countless homes ... decorations will be hung, cards posted, and phone calls made, all of which form part of the annual reminder of the birth of Christ.

These should be days of joy for the world. And no matter what faith or religion in which you believe or follow, peace should reign. Hope and love ought to resonate and echo within every heart and home, too. Contentment for, and of, who and what you are, can then elevate you all above doubt and fear. This enables humanity to connect through body, mind, and spirit ... but will it?

In these hectic moments, many areas of one's life can attempt to divert and side-track you away from the truth and me. The commercial pressure, with materialism and the expenditure of money, brings both stress and disease to the mind and the household. Yet for some, there aren't such choices. They don't have worries over which party clothes to wear, as they just simply wish to find somewhere to sleep or some food to eat.

Understand please, this 'lesson will not turn into (and what some may call) a guilt trip. Nor relayed to you in the desire to make you feel any different from what you already do, that's unless you wish to. Only you can determine change within or without the 'self.' No amount of persuasion can alter that, just like someone who sees obstructions to a diet, getting fit, or becoming educated through additional training. Remember, 'you can lead a horse to water but you cannot make it drink.'

Realise too, around the world, conflict, malnutrition, anger, hate, and fear cross continents like an airborne virus. Only by utilizing the filters of non-discrimination, compassion, and discernment can you all make the correct choices and decisions to transfer and dilute such negativity. This will bring a new calmness to humanity and Mother Earth.

So, having woken upon this new day, are you grateful for your sleep, whilst having the ability to even rise from your bed? When you opened your eyes, is there gratitude for seeing the alarm clock, while there are others who have no sight. Then, as you dress, putting on extra clothes for warmth upon a cold winter's day, can you spare a thought for those who walk half-naked on their own road and journey of experience? When you wash your face and clean your teeth with clean water—perhaps leaving the tap running—does a notion trickle down from the mind and into your heart … for those who pray for just a single sip to quench their thirst?

Don't be sad. Please comprehend that love is stronger than all other things, and so it will prevail, though you must want it to. Can you? Now consider the Christmas dinner table this year. Will you be grateful for the luxury of choice and the food to eat, be it savoury or sweet? Would you know if a friend, neighbour, or even a stranger in the same street (or across the world) goes without, or eats scraps to survive? Yes indeed, while 80% of the world thrives, are the rest denied, with tears … asking how and why?

Do you feel blessed to have the love of a friend, a father, mother, sister, brother, or even a loyal and beloved pet? Appreciate also, there are those who sit or walk seemingly alone, feeling neglected by kith and kin, by society, the state or country, and even the world.

For those I speak of, I say and tell you ... I walk with every step you take. And know this ... I hold your hands while I place your hearts within my own. I cradle you within my grace, of which I pour over your souls to eternally sustain you. Whilst you may often feel the world has abandoned you, realise you are not—and never can be—a stranger to me, as we are forever 'one'.

Those without a bed, whether through one's own karma and experience, shall lie down in my fields of peace. The fragrance of my divine essence will lift thy heart to magical planes ... beyond the fear and dread of the night and cold. The emptiness of belly, please understand, is only temporary. I will fulfil you within and out by sitting at my table—within the Kingdom of Heaven—nourished by trust, belief, and an unwavering faith.

Right now, may every one of you count your blessing this Christmas time. Be grateful for whatever mercy is placed there for you. Do not doubt yourself to become even brighter next year, to shine and share the truth within. May you become the true you for all those you encounter upon the Earth ... whether that's in your own thoughts, through spoken word, or even upon the ether in your dreams whist you sleep. Blessed be, Amen."

We each took a deep breath and became still, and silent, for what was to come. I clinked the glass of water on the table with the edge of the spoon, and embarked on our thirty minutes of silent meditation.

Almost instantly, Sai entered the room, this time wearing a red robe ... poignant for this special time of year. It was as if He was acknowledging such. As I gazed upon him, he sort of half-turned to the right and waved His right arm to the side. He brought forth a magical scene and disappeared from view within a flurry of falling snow. Reindeer approached. Everything was peaceful. Santa Claus was here ... and stood before us, within radiating light and love. He spoke in a deep, yet loving, voice. "I come bearing gifts ... and to rejoice in the birth of the Lord!"

He walked over to Jill, and placed a yellow/golden box in her hands. It signifies God's grace and illumination. It is wrapped with a scarlet ribbon, symbolising the energy contained therein. It is opened. "You find the utensils inside ... for a kitchen. This relates to something you are concocting ... with the ingredients of life. Like a cake mixture, you have everything you need inside of you, to bring forth the goodness that others can partake in (from you) ... kindness and truth and light. From your own efforts, you can nourish and sustain those whom you meet. Everything that you need (remember), is already within you."

Santa hands Keith his present. It's a green and red box, for healing and energy. A golden ribbon elegantly wraps the parcel ... symbolising God's grace. "Please open it." Keith opens it, embracing his inner child's anticipation and glee. "These earphones are a gift ... so that you can hear and understand, the true sound of silence. They are also protection from unwanted background noise and hearsay, which can detract you from recognition of the truth. Listen and hear God speaking through your surroundings ... birdsong, the rustling of wind in the branches of the trees, or water flowing down a stream. When you are still, you know the truth inside your heart."

He turns towards Kimmy and places a weird shaped parcel, wrapped in gold paper (God's grace) and a beautiful blue ribbon (for protection) in her lap. She opens it and finds a bat, like a table tennis paddle. "This present is to help you return the service that you are ... and have completed. (A return of serve). This provides the extra ability and energy to 'rally' against those who wish or need to play the 'game'. It is the strength to earn one's own victory."

In the centre of the room—on a small 'occasional' table—there's a glass of milk, and a small plate mince pies. Father Christmas drinks the milk of human kindness, then eats a mince pie. He takes another for the reindeer. He turns to wave goodbye and says," Nourishment is shared, like loving words to fulfil and sustain you all, for the continued journey ahead … and the tasks yet to be completed. Peace and goodwill to all."

A glow of brilliant orange appears behind him like a brilliant sunset, and the snow flurries have disappeared. It feels like all seasons in one day. I comprehend this is Sai's continuing presence … a present for us all no matter what life brings … come rain or shine. Amen to that. Thank you, thank you, thank you. Om Sai Ram.

Shortly after, I could see the clock, and that the meditation period was almost over. I paused for a moment, waiting for the others to centre themselves, returning from their own experiences. I said a closing prayer of thanks and blessings. Keith had recently found a small doves feather in his garden. We used this to share any spiritual messages received either for, or through, each devotee. I read what was transcribed, which was magical indeed.

We chanted the final mantra of that year:

> ***"Lokah Samastah Sukhino Bhavantu,***
> ***Lokah Samastah Sukhino Bhavantu,***
> ***Lokah Samastah Sukhino Bhavantu***
>
> ***Shanti, Shanti, Shanti!"***

I helped Keith make the tea … and then we all laughed when he brought through a large plate of mince pies and biscuits! What a lovely way to conclude the Circle. We will all be forever grateful for everything that God has allowed us to experience and share through

Sai, Jesus, our spirit guides and all those in the heavenly realms and dimensions.

It was nearly ten o'clock, and time to head home. Praise be to God in the highest, for such a magical year of divine guidance. Om Sai Ram/Amen.

In another December Circle meeting, when we gathered at Keith's home, winter was really starting to set in. It was bitterly cold and frosty outside. I had picked Jill up on the way, and though short on numbers when we arrived, we'd later find out that Baba would share the most wonderful symbolism and messages again for us all.

We settled down with a hot cup of tea and a chat, before offering a prayer of protection and guidance. The candle and incense were lit. We all chanted the mantra before reading a lesson to the group.

> *"Aum Bhur Bhurvah Suvah*
> *Tat Savitur Varenyam*
> *Bhargo Devasya Dheemahi*
> *Dhiyo yonah Prachodayat."*

Lesson: **HISTORY (HIS-STORY)**

"The physical heart of your body beats like a drum—many times per minute—but the flame and radiating coil at the seat of your soul resonates many more per second. In a similar fashion, this life-giving organ enables your blood to be cleansed and circulated around the body. It brings vital protection and nutrients to every fibre, sinew, muscle, and veins. Meanwhile, the illumination of love from your spark of divinity provides power as it flows and pulses with beams of energy so finite, only the vision of body, mind, and soul in unison can see it.

Like a mirror, this reflects from both the inside and out. Therefore, everyone notices when their body 'surface' changes—as if you are wearing different clothes throughout the seasons of one's life—whether that's during childhood, your youth, and teenage years, and into middle and old age. The inner flame, however, reflects true character and personality, along with the knowledge, experience, and wisdom of the soul, through every thought, word, and deed, but who can comprehend this?

How many of you recognize your own traits and qualities, or dare I say, perhaps your own faults, too? In addition, at what point would one realise the consequences of their actions, which affect those far beyond the walls in which they live?

Often, someone will think they can do no wrong, but on the other hand, one may feel they can do no right either! Well, I can help you then, by asking you to imagine you had a two-way mirror, so you could see in a different light. You could even demand to know what is real, or are you guilty of something which you can only ever ask of yourself?

As you are your own judge and jury, this is your own decision to make. What is more intriguing occurs in the recognition of such, since it allows you to access reality, which enables you to question the 'confined', the informant, the 'one' who is held until the truth 'will out'.

Please comprehend it is 'I' who am your captive … or that I am 'captivated' by your essence and the power of your love. I am a 'model' prisoner, though, because I serve you freely, wantonly, and willingly, without exception.

So, where have I been and where can I go? Well, if I am under a non-physical lock and key, this can only represent true love and light. Recognize the two co-exist as one, and by that, we can deem them 'unfit for purpose' or, are an amazing combination, linked forever into eternity.

Try to create a new scene within your mind and picture this two-way mirror ... which now lets you observe me, to state, "You only require the truth, and then you will release me". But will you? Could you free me from your heart, so I can bear witness to the reflection, which shines from all those whom you meet and greet?

Do not get angry or become frustrated with me, either. Those feelings only block out what I am trying to tell you ... and prevents love from entering your soul, which in turn leads the hands to action. Therefore, you want the truth, the whole truth and nothing but the truth ... do you?

"Yes, I do. So where were you?"

I am everywhere.

"Ok, now tell me, what did you take from me?"

I took all your sins.

"Why?"

Well, by clearing your karma, you find balance. When you obtain balance, you will discover contentment and peace. Recognizing peace through 'self-realization', you enter bliss. Once here, you appreciate you are truly 'home' ... forever beside, within, without, above, and below me.

"I hear what you're saying, God, but that's just part of history, right?"

No, that's 'His-Story' … the way, the truth, and the light.

"How can I believe you … that what you are telling me is true?"

What other proof do you need—or want?

"Maybe we all want a miracle. Yes, that's it … we do! We need something we can all witness with our own eyes, and not what happened in texts of old within lots of different religions and faiths around the world."

You are 'it'.

"What's that supposed to mean?"

You are the miracle.

"Eh? I'm confused."

Do not be. Now you're taking off the rose-coloured spectacles, you can re-focus through the lens of your heart, because you know I exist.

"I do?"

Of course … we're both talking, aren't we?

"Oh, but how do I know it's not all a trick?"

Why would I do that, you are the one with the key, remember?

"Alright, so the miracle is 'I'?"

Yes. For you neither recognized your true self, nor the power inside you. Please comprehend, this allows you to choose not only how to live, but to love and shine, too. How else can you keep me hidden for so long?

"Okay, okay, okay. So, what you are saying then, is you're the innocent one in all this?"

No, not at all ... only that guilt and blame hold no place in your heart, and because you were not living the truth, by acting from—and seeing with—your heart ... you had forgotten who and what you are.

"And, that is?"

That you are already 'free'. Please remember, all the while you believed it is I, fighting to break out, but I wasn't. You imagined the body was all there is, hence, you were trapping your own 'self'. In doing so, you could not sense me.

"In fact, I can't even recall how I got you in here, so I could ask you these things."

I was here before you even 'existed' ... for I was, am and forever will be, and now you will be too.

"I'm beginning to understand. You are love ... and I am too, right?"

Of course.

"So, what do I do now?"

Release me. It must be you who sets me free in order to let me work through you and your heart.

"Will I need to change anything?"

Only your thoughts, as they often hold you back. Think, and then feel, share, be, and act from and through and to love. You might find this difficult at first, but you will learn from any mistakes. So, do not fear, because any consequences will be my burden if you try to live in truth.

"Huh, you've just handed me a 'get out of jail free' card!"

No, it is you who gives it to me.

"Thank you, God. I will need to write this into the record book now, as anyone else who brings you in for questioning can save time and effort ... the truth written for all to see."

Indeed, that may help many.

"What do you want me to do now?"

I do not need or want you to do anything ... other than to be your actual self. You are the miracle, remember. Believe in yourself and make your life a happy one by making your dreams come true. I am working with, through, in, and from you, as I have always tried to do.

The only difference is that you now comprehend us as 'one'. The false separation of the two needed to be dispelled, especially when the heart has yearned for more than everyday life, much more than just eating, working, and sleeping. In recognizing there was—and is—more to life than yourself, you'll know what is real, bringing history and 'His-Story' of the past, through to the present, and for a bright new future.

Realise we are connected by chains of love and light, and those magical cords of truth, into eternity. Therefore, be who you were born to be and do not waste time and become fulfilled in the knowledge you are already free.

Illuminate and shine all you are and can be from 'within'. Before long, others will remember their own reality and understand their own 'history' to reveal my gift, which I pre-sent to carry you every day, through the future, and throughout the eons of time. Amen."

After the reading, everyone was comfortable and settled. We then engaged in a few minutes of deep breath work, before the meditation … and thirty minutes of wonderful silence.

I picked up my notepad and pen just as Swami appeared. Once again, he was wearing his saffron gown, yet behind His crown of hair, a brilliant white glow emerged. I knew it was the connection to Jesus that He was bringing through with Him.

With a wave of his right hand the room became filled with a winter scene. Snowflakes, brilliant white and soft were gently falling. Christmas day was not too far away. From his crown, an old fashioned Christmas decoration, a multi-coloured paperchain began to form, and circle above our heads. It signified His connection to Lord Jesus and indeed, every religion of 'man' … and to each of us, too. He spoke, "This chain represents that all are one. Your karma is connected to your soul's journey and encompasses your present and future … and your past/ history too. You could even say that yes, it's 'His-Story' too."

Sai looked over to Jill, and from the swirling paperchain above, a piece of the paperchain looped over her head, like a Christmas cracker hat! "You are receiving the colour blue … for healing that you require and send."

Gazing over to Keith, another segment of the chain sat on his head. "I give you the colour orange, for assimilation, to merge into me." Turning to face Kimmy, a bright yellow loop sat directly over her, dropping down to her forehead "I provide a yellow link, to enhance your intuition. It is important to listen to that gut feeling … and your heart."

After a brief pause, Sai spoke again. " The path that you each tread can leave a temporary or permanent trace. The former, like footprints covered over by a fresh flurry of snow. The latter, however, resembles steps into soft soil ... and the overnight frost helps to provide a lasting impression. Know that your love that shines wherever you go, can be the legacy to help nurture or inspire others, and hence, it will not fade or lead them astray. That said, your path is no one else's, and vice versa. This is why each so-journ (soul journey), is unique for every one of you. Remember, you are linked as one, and nothing can ever detract from that."

Suddenly, a Christmas tree appeared by Sai's side. No decorations were needed as the pine needles and branches were beautiful in their own right. They emitted their own luminosity, far greater than man-made fairy lights could ever do. My heart gasped, as the a crucifix began to form on the top of the tree. Then, the Lord's face seemed to envelope the cross and illuminated the room ... as a 'figurehead'. Swami spoke, "All can bear witness if they can see with the lens of truth ... the eye of the body, soul and mind as one."

The faint snowdrops finally stopped falling. As I looked upwards, the ceiling had disappeared, to reveal a clear night sky. Stars ... the universe ... Creation. Baba waved His right hand once more, as if to say goodbye. As he disappeared from view he said, "Know the birth and life of Christ is one journey, and yet all journeys. It is through self-realization one enters true bliss and peace. Amen."

I clinked the edge of a glass of water with a tea spoon, signalling the end of the meditation. Amazing! What a privilege, and most wonderful experience indeed. We closed the circle with some absent healing and prayers, then chanted the Lokah Samastah mantra:

"Lokah Samastah Sukhino Bhavantu,
Lokah Samastah Sukhino Bhavantu,
Lokah Samastah Sukhino Bhavantu

Shanti, Shanti, Shanti!"

Over another hot drink, Kimmy, Jill and Keith, shared their meditations experiences, and I read the transcribed notes that I had made too. We offered Sai and Jesus our sincere gratitude for their grace and presence and Divine guidance. Om Sai Ram/ Amen! Then, after saying our goodbye's, a slow drive home followed, with all our hearts feeling blessed, beyond measure! Praise be to God.

It is nearly Christmas, and ten devotees are sitting for tonight's circle. It's amazing that we can gather in this way ... celebrating Jesus's forthcoming birthday, and hopefully, Swami's divine guidance and presence once more!

We sat comfortably, and readied ourselves for the spiritual work to begin. Some simply closed their eyes, others calmed their bodies and minds with some breathing exercises. Robert said an opening prayer, then we all followed with the Gayathri Mantra:

"Aum Bhur Bhurvah Suvah
Tat Savitur Varenyam
Bhargo Devasya Dheemahi
Dhiyo yonah Prachodayat."

CHRISTMAS AND SPIRITUAL 'GIFTS'

I then read the following lesson: **PEACE AND GOODWILL**

"Love and light and truth and kindness flow to each one of you, but what you are and can yet become still depends upon your thoughts, words and deeds. Would you say this is your own freewill, or by the Divinity within you, which enables you to shine more brightly, offering peace and balance to those whom you meet?

I state this so you do not think relationships, acquaintances, or meetings of like minds happen by chance, when in fact you are often guided to go where you are needed most … both your own and for another's experiences. Consider this not as fate, but the pathway to greater things.

Please understand too, although words such as destiny, nirvana, and bliss try to describe one's journey and goal, everything you say carries the power to either uplift another's heart … or when spoken in anger—or with hate—cut down the very soul, which reflects your own and me. Therefore, by seeing the divinity in everything, you are bearing witness to your true 'self' too.

In reality, when also assisting and helping others, spirals of energy—formed through love and light—swirl from inside and above you, like a DNA helix both touching and melting within the vibration and resonance of creation. These can travel through all dimensions, time, and space, far beyond your phenomenal world and earth-plane too. It is a fact, not fiction, when coming from a true heart. Nothing can erase or break it in two, for it is all pervading.

Right now, many of you are preparing for Christmas, which is a season for peace and goodwill. However, as I mentioned once before, this can be a worrying period for many reasons, not least to those whose hearts radiate with despair, frustration, or fear. In most situations though, a helping hand is all it takes to lighten the load, or by offering forgiveness and compassion, give strength and hope to another ... but in whatever form, know this gesture is a spark, re-igniting the peace to flourish inside a heart.

Remember, if you assist in truth, not only does the recipient benefit, so do those who gather and witness the event too. This is because kindness indirectly magnifies within the aura and timeless energy surrounding it. Do not become confused or misinterpret these things, though, because our connection is eternal, sustained by the 'to and fro' of a beating heart of light.

Please try to become more aware of such opportunities, as 'looking' with physical eyes alone; they often pass unnoticed. Overall, by living a life of unconditional love, everything opens up before you. In fact, what then evolves in and around you are so magnificent that some regard as miracles in themselves.

What do you need to do in order to activate these wonderful things? Well, why speak when a smile or hug can show how much you care. Ask yourself right now, when someone crawls upon hands and knees in total despair, and their heart and soul seem torn in two, what can you do?

I urge your love to draw closer, and let it be a candle of light within their darkest hour. Shine forth like a beacon and draw back the veil of illusion and bewildering pain of confusion, which entraps and grounds them. May your kindness be there when it's needed most, and if you believe it to be true, it will be, I promise you. (The recognition of this gracious act may not be perceived straight away but is felt far beyond the senses of the people close by).

In terms of one's development, their personal journey and quest, you will always find me 'inside' your heart ... where peace and goodwill reign supreme; and nothing can detract from this. By searching within, one can be happiest and most content you can ever be, and this does not exist upon the phenomenal world, as nothing is permanent there. In stillness, you discover we are forever ... eternal and everlasting, and with a true understanding of being 'one' without separation or division. Such joy can, and will, radiate for all, and only the 'timing' taking place on the earth-plane detracts from this.

Therefore, what do the masses wish and yearn for at this festive time? Many hearts will cry out, "I want peace"—in the belief it is previously unattainable—but take away the ego (I), the desire (want) ... and they will leave you with peace. So too, by removing the immorality you have immortality, and goodwill transcends to 'God's' will.

One must comprehend there is no need to suffer or fear at all, just have faith in yourself and not in false desires or greed. Share your limitless love, and you will see the effects upon the lives of those around you, and indeed, also on your own.

Please try to see the beauty and the magnificence of the truth, as the light within shall reveal the golden path which leads you to me. I am always waiting and never hiding, and my open heart and arms will cradle you in bliss ... all you have to do is believe, as I have said so many times before.

> Know me, like I know you,
> Want me, like I want you,
> Trust me, like I trust you,
> Understand me, like I understand you,
> Believe in me, like I believe in you.
> Then truly discover me, your secret treasure,
> Keeping me close, for we are 'one'.
> Remember me always, in all things said and done,
> No separation, no division, and just become.
> Amen."

After the above reading, Robert gave a swift single chime of the table bell for the meditation to begin. I picked up my notepad and pen, in great anticipation of Sai's appearance, which I had prayed would come to fruition. After a brief moment, He stood in the centre of the circle, this time dressed in His brilliant white robe, which shimmered and sparkled as if it was reflecting sunlight. Swami raised His right hand, and said, "Happy, happy, happy…" He then clasped both His hands together near His waist, and looked towards Issy. I knew right away, that He was going to present everyone in the circle with a precious gift.

Issy: Sai placed a white garland over her head. It rested precisely over her heart. "This is for honour and service and peace, and the Unity of Faiths."

Keith: Swami unfurls a small white flag, with a red sun in its centre. "This symbolises the rising sun (and 'Son') within you … to illuminate and shine for others to see."

Kimmy was sitting with her open hands on her lap. Baba raises his hands. Blue petals, softer than the finest silk, pour forth … falling into her hands. "They contain the fragrance of my Divine essence, and through working hands … heal."

Julie: Sai presents a vibrant 'Robin' red headscarf, adorned with holly. "The reason behind the headscarf is two-fold. Firstly to prick your conscience, and give you a nudge when required. Secondly, the Robin redbreast reference is for elevation … and beautiful birdsong for angelic resonance and protection."

Manny: An old school wooden ruler is placed in Manny's right hand. "To help you measure out/distance yourself from negative influences. It will also provide you with a 'rule of thumb' … to distinguish and observe the difference between the obvious, and what seems hidden below the surface."

Robert: Swami materialises a magnifying glass 'out of thin air'. "This will assist you in closing in, and to focus upon the minute details ... bringing information, insight, inspiration, and new knowledge to be shared—and for inner growth."

Jim: Sai presents Jim with an empty birdcage. "This signifies having flown the next ... your soul taking flight. There are no barriers ... mental freedom. Your mind and consciousness is no longer restricted."

Kate: "I give you this flower, an orange daffodil. It's stem is your body. The outer petals are your mind. The centre is your heart and soul. Forget time ... spring now into divine action. Be aware of the opportunity to bloom and display your love in all its glory."

Baba returned to the centre of the circle and continued to smile. (When one witnessed His smile, it was as if the world's ills and pain would instantly evaporate ... all through the depths of His love). He raised His right arm to make me aware the meeting was over, and promptly disappeared into the ether.

Out of the corner of my eye, Robert reached for the bell, the thirty minutes of silence had ended. Divine timing indeed! It took a few minutes for everyone to feel grounded again. Robert said a closing prayer of gratitude. Each person took the white feather in turn, and shared what they had experienced. When I received the feather, it felt very emotional. I clasped it tightly and eagerly proceeded to share Swami's divine love and guidance and spiritual gifts.

We closed the circle with the Lokah Samastah mantra:

"Lokah Samastah Sukhino Bhavantu,
Lokah Samastah Sukhino Bhavantu,
Lokah Samastah Sukhino Bhavantu

Shanti, Shanti, Shanti!"

It took a few minutes for everyone to come to terms with such blessings and grace that had been bestowed upon us all. Such wonder and peace is hard to describe. We gave our humble thanks to our beloved Sai and shared some Vibhuti.

Kate and Robert had laid food out on the dining room table, prior to the circle ... which we duly tucked into! After a cup of tea we all departed for home. What a brilliant evening. Till next time ... thank you, beloved Sai and dear Lord Jesus ... praise be to God. Om Sai Ram/Amen.

SYMBOLISM AND COLOUR

It was a very cold, frosty evening. The 21 miles drive to Peterborough took longer than usual, but I was treated to nature's splendour along some countryside roads. As car lights passed by, they lit up the icy verges, which appeared to sparkle like diamonds or glistening stars within the heavens above me.

Upon arrival, the warmth of Robert's and Kate's home was truly a blessing, and with a cup of tea, I soon warmed up. Normal proceedings followed, and I looked forward to the mediation tonight … in the hope that Sai would continue to bless us with his presence and grace. Robert's opening prayer proceeded the Circle chanting the Gayathri Mantra:

>*"Aum Bhur Bhurvah Suvah*
>*Tat Savitur Varenyam*
>*Bhargo Devasya Dheemahi*
>*Dhiyo yonah Prachodayat."*

After a few mins silence, I gave the following reading to the group.

Lesson: **FROST**

"Welcome to thy peace, stillness, and warmth of my loving heart once more. Now, as the outside temperature drops, it brings forth a winter's chill, ... and enables you to experience the first real frost of the season. With it, a crisp veil of ice has formed. It resembles a carpet of silver and white glitter, and everything around you is being transformed—as if by magic—and nothing escapes its vice like grip.

You gaze upon it, so why not venture outside, and try something new? Perhaps you could walk barefoot on the lawn? If you do, the coolness may shock your feet at first, but sensations rising through you will make you feel truly alive. You will also hear those tiny sound vibrations as your weight squashes the icy particles below you, and these echo and reverberate over many levels.

So too, as the coldness is recognized, and the realization hits your brain, it instantaneously alerts you to this drastic change in temperature. Then, once you leave the grass, the exact opposite occurs. Your feet respond from the numbness, you will certainly become alert and uplifted.

In comparison, how often do you bare your sole(s)/soul to sudden changes in your surroundings? What conditions are you prepared to be exposed to? And just like the frosty lawn, would you undertake these willingly to experiencing the rawness, and for your heart to become immersed in new challenges and ways of being?

Only you can determine and answer such things. But be honest with yourself as you endeavour to walk upon your own road or path. Then, when it is time for you to 'cross over', there is no need to pause, reflect or wish for a chance to turn back the clock ... because of regrets, or a desire to erase those doubts of so-called missed opportunities.

To do so is like viewing your steps left behind in the frosted lawn. They may appear to resemble real tracks—a residue of where you have been—but unless you walk in, and through and from, and to love … the experiences will eventually fade. Those footprints soon melt away when the sun (and Son) rises above you.

How can you leave a more permanent legacy? What reminder, what memory and treasure can you store within friends, family, and neighbour's hearts and minds? You cannot find the answer in your home, car or the possessions you accumulate upon the Earth. No. Only your love is real and eternal, which is portrayed through one's character and personality.

As I explained many times before, try to be self-less, not selfish. Live with those true human qualities such as truth, non-violence, and righteousness. I do not command or require you to be anything other than what you already are. Only by understanding and knowing your real self … will you reflect your own divinity.

Therefore, with your day now in motion, what choices did you make? Have you earmarked all your time to embark upon one's toils? Or can you set aside a moment for you, me, and us? Remember, one cannot, or should not, underestimate the moments spent within peace and reflection, especially in the era of such a fast-paced and demanding society of which you are all part. Indeed, remain in the world, but do not believe you are what the world is, separated from your true self and me.

Moving on from this, one's environment can appear dull and withered during winter, so it is prudent to view through different lenses. Unlike those three-dimensional (3D) glasses, which attempt to imitate real life on a television screen, please look and feel with your heart instead.

This will bring new and pleasant surprises every day. For instance, birds still fly and sing, while a tree—even without leaves—draws one to the beauty of its bark. Also, when conditions are exactly right, a full moon in the coldness of night will cause the rooftops to shimmer and shine like mirrors ... while hedgerows and verges sparkle like stardust, as car headlights compete with nature's rays of light.

One must realise, as you make your way through the journey of your life and soul, there are those whose hearts are frozen. Coming across individuals or groups of people with chilled emotions may often prove difficult. Therefore, please see these not as obstacles or challenges, but fresh opportunities to melt hardened feelings with kindness and gratitude.

Others can be difficult to talk to, work alongside, or even become friends with. They resemble hearts coated in candy sugar. They are both very sweet and nice, but under this exterior layer—deep inside—lurks anger, frustration, and many fears. On the other hand, if the heart is plainly good and a joy to be near, the thin protective shield surrounding it, may wish to stop many emotions, thoughts, and feelings from entering, and as such prefers a self-imposed solitude upon itself.

Be delicate. Tread carefully when interacting with a heart like this. Some are so fragile from their own grief or pain, or from living in their own struggle to make sense of life and the world, that one sharp word, action or thought, can crack the ice, penetrating deep within.

Please refrain from attempting to break this too soon. Do not force attitudes or beliefs on another, as all life must keep the choice of whom, what or why they believe in someone or something. Indeed, they may require gently thawing instead, so their own development can flourish like a flower bulb, peering through the surface of the ground as and when spring appears. In fact, why not ask yourself, "Am I prepared? Do I wish to learn and grow within and 'without' this mortal coil?"

Well, just like an overcoat—which tries to protect you from the cold—the body wants to adjust and adapt to its different situations and conditions it finds itself in. Too hot and you will sweat. The body releases what it doesn't need, but the soul also wishes to attain balance, removing karmic debt where it can, so the overcoat or 'body' will no longer be required either. Do not think in terms of becoming exposed. Rather, you are a living, burning flame of immense strength, enabling other hands and souls to find you for healing, direction, and purpose.

For this reason, know my love 'lights' the way for you when all other lights dim or fade away. Remember, the frost is but a temporary condition. So now move forward in the knowledge both warmth and comfort are only a heartbeat away. Amen."

The room was quiet and still, and with the faintest of chimes from the table bell, the meditation began. I could feel the energy building within and around me. I picked up my pen and notepad with great anticipation.

Swami 'entered' the room, and stood in front of the fireplace. His hands began to swirl and Vibhuti springled all across the room. "This ash is my body, my light and divine essence. It cleanses and eradicates harmful energy, and brings peace to all those who gather in my name. We are all one." He moved in front of each member of the Circle in turn, and relayed his guidance through me...

Manny: "Welcome once more dear child. Through your heart, you stay connected with mine at all times. Know that when the glow of the Sun appears and disappears over the horizon, my love still shines eternally within you."

Keith: "Like a mirror, reflect the love that lays within your heart and soul. Let it be a sign and signal to attract those who are distant or who seem to distance themselves away from the truth. Illuminate the path for others to follow."

Kimmy: "Your spark of divinity is pure and true. Those you come into contact with contain the same but their light is hidden by fear and worry. Clean the illusion away from their hearts through love and truth, so that they can recognise the glory of their true selves."

Jan: "My dear sweet child, the plumes of thy heart send the fragrance of our love to those in need. It is not important to know when or where, for like a seed upon the wind … my breath of life directs it precisely when they require it to do so. May peace descend upon thee."

Kate: Kindness flows through your blood and veins like our love that extends beyond the physical body through thought and prayer. What you feel inside is real, and the reality and truth emanates from the same. Let your light flow far and wide from deep within your soul. Know that there are no boundaries to prevent our connection, and therefore there is no one and nothing that your love cannot reach or touch."

Issy: "The energy of truth and love shall permeate through your mind and heart. In every physical sojourn memories may come and go, but our connection and the love in your heart remains constant for all time. Do not worry or fear, as you are mine."

As the meditation period was drawing to a close, Baba turned away with a wave and softly whispered, "All Love … Love all."

I would often feel very emotional during His visits/messages. Sometimes tears would fall down my cheeks as I transcribed what was being shared. Everything comes through Him, because of His grace and blessings.

Salutations and absent healing and prayers followed and we concluded the meeting with the Lokah Samastah. Circle:

"Lokah Samastah Sukhino Bhavantu,
Lokah Samastah Sukhino Bhavantu,
Lokah Samastah Sukhino Bhavantu

Shanti, Shanti, Shanti!

I shared Swami's messages followed by each devotee in turn with the white feather. Kate and Robert treated us with hot food like Samosas, onion Bhaji's, along with other nibbles such as crisps, tea and cake. A real feast. Tonight was such an awesome Circle/meeting indeed. Thanks be to God! Om Sai Ram … Amen.

On this particular evening, seven devotees were present. I arrived about fifteen minutes early, plenty of time to have a lovely cup of tea and a chat before the circle started. It had been a hectic day, so I felt I needed to clear my mind and calm my breathing rate down in preparation for the stillness to come. Everyone made themselves comfortable. Robert said a prayer for love and healing, before we all chanted the Gayathri Mantra.

"Aum Bhur Bhurvah Suvah
Tat Savitur Varenyam
Bhargo Devasya Dheemahi
Dhiyo yonah Prachodayat."

I read the lesson: **BEING 'STILL' IN THE WEB OF LIFE**

"Welcome, once again. Please understand, the depths of one's heart may reveal an abyss of uncertainty and doubt, or in contrast, amazing peace and bliss. Therefore, while you seek and search within yourself, you can grow and learn much more than you believe was ever possible. Do you desire and really wish this? Or, are you afraid of what you will discover of your true self? Simply being aware of the choices you are making (and their resulting actions), will all have an effect upon you.

Regarding your goals and aspirations, people experience anxiety and frustration by deeming them as good, bad, or indifferent, but this not only influences your own way and path, but those of others who are close by and (seemingly), far away too.

In fact, your thoughts, words, and deeds enable such seeds to be sown and nurtured, allowing real growth and fulfilment. On the other hand, perhaps they will flounder, with one's hopes, dreams and wishes swirling inside the heart … like a feather, carried upon a gust of wind with no resting place. Remember, roots of a tree flourish with soil and water, and likewise, your strength of conviction and character can ground you and set you gently in place, where you can then contemplate and become still.

As I have stated on numerous occasions, this helps you reflect the truth both 'within' and out, to shine like a beacon, instead of a tiny spark or ember. Realise too, your divinity is a living flame of my love and light, of such beauty and majestic brilliance, these words cannot portray.

Countless souls and beings across many eras of history (and through vast planes and dimensions of energy), dampen their essence and divine spark because of unbalanced karma. Nonetheless, do not feel time is running out, though it is vital for you to rekindle the fire … in order to expand in both wisdom and knowledge.

Through kindness and love, you can share with those who open their own hearts and minds, helping others to grow and know who they are, and what they will become. Destiny is truth—and truth is destiny—and currently, you cannot mature spiritually or consciously, without the experience of being in human 'form'. Please understand, through one's journey over many lifetimes (and the endeavours of mind and heart), piece by piece, the darkness of 'ego' and the lower self shall fall away. Please realise that…

> You are all connected by strands of light and love,
> While a soul is never 'born', from within or up above.
> So, you yearn and try to search, from both heart and then your mind,
> But I reveal you're so much more … not alone or one of kind.
>
> Like the spider's web vibrating, upon and in the wind,
> Fragments of life are 'captured', so do you think that you have sinned?
> Yes, nourishment for one, and maybe fear and pain another,
> While the experience is for all, of this you now discover.
>
> In the centre it connects, as each link then forms a line,
> A web of life to live … in truth and you will be fine.
> Because energy is forever, and this cannot be changed,
> Only those who do not learn … will think it all in vain.
>
> Think of it right now, upon a cold and frosty morn,
> It glistens and it glows, as the Sun begins to warm.
> Frozen elements they do cling, from the deep and dead of night,
> And in a quiet pause of stillness, do you long to now take flight?

For peace and now this truth, will melt all those hardened thoughts,
Captured by frames of time, you had believed they could be bought.
Not by money or material, or any false and earthbound pleasure,
   The golden centre of all life ... I reveal as your true treasure.

   So, know you are not trapped ... or enclosed to be passed by,
   For growth and understanding, means the higher you can fly.
With knowledge now move on, and glow brightly as the 'Son',
   Live eternally in peace, forever you and I as one. Amen."

After the reading, we sat still for a minute or so ... before Robert gave a single chime of the bell. The thirty minutes of tranquillity had begun. My notepad and pen were ready, for I felt sure Sai would bless us with His grace and love tonight. Almost immediately, Sai appeared in front of the fireplace. Beloved Sai Geeta, proudly stood by His side ... her trunk gently swaying side to side and up and down with a trumpet salute. This was surely our protection for the evening. Thank you Baba and Sai Geeta!

Suddenly, Swami stood in front of me, and placed a golden crown upon my head. He then materialised the same for each of the circle. I felt immensely humbled to receive such a gift. Sai spoke, "A crown can signify many things. One may consider the following words, and deem them all to be associated with such ... regal, majestic, royal, kingdom, king, unity and glory. However, with duty comes the responsibility ... to be shining examples of my love."

Swami turned towards Keith and presented him with a toothpick! "This will provide spiritual help ... and enable you to remove any impediments and discomfort of the spoken word. Food too, can contain harmful bacteria. One can compare this with the non-spiritual voice of unreason."

Sai raised his right hand, waved it once in a circle, and a silver thimble fell straight down into Keith's lap. "This will provide protection … from that which pricks your conscious mind. It is precious metal … or rather 'me-to-all'."

Kimmy: "I give you a knitting needle. Remember, 'a stitch in time saves nine'. You now have a greater ability to weave and link together … those less fortunate."

Julie: Lots of elastic bands, suddenly appeared on Julie's right arm. "These have a multitude of uses. They will give you the extra flexibility to bind and link together … those who draw close, even if they are confused."

Kate: Baba places a pair of scissors in her lap. "These will assist you, to cut through the red tape of your own democracy and indecision … which may try to lead and deviate you from your new and chosen path of truth."

Jim: "I place an eternity ring upon your finger. This represents our unity, our 'oneness' … a union with the Father/Mother God. This is an internal vow, made since your souls creation. No division or separation, remember?"

Sai stepped back into the centre of the circle. He then pulled a single hair from His beautiful 'crown'. This began to float in the air, like a wisp of silk towards us all. It became a web of life. Swami's arm began to wave in a circle, and as He and Sai Geeta disappeared, said, "We are one."

Wow … that was incredible! I placed down my pen. Within a few seconds Robert rang the table bell for the meditation to close. It took a few minutes before everyone had recognised their physical bodies once more. After a brief pause, Jim picked up the white feather and shared his 'messages', then the rest of the Circle followed. I then read my notes of Baba's divine guidance for each devotee.

Robert said a brief closing prayer of gratitude, and we all sent absent healing to family, friends and the world. The meeting ended with the Lokah Samastah mantra:

"Lokah Samastah Sukhino Bhavantu,
Lokah Samastah Sukhino Bhavantu,
Lokah Samastah Sukhino Bhavantu

Shanti, Shanti, Shanti!"

Robert then shared Vibhuti with us all. Afterwards, he and Kate served the evening snacks on the dining table, and these went down a treat with cups of tea and coffee. What an amazing circle tonight, a great privilege indeed. Thank you beloved Baba, and Sai Geeta. Om Sai Ram/Amen. Praise be to God in the highest!

The following months circle was yet another inspirational meeting. I always hoped to be there about 7.45pm for the 8.00 pm start, but no matter what time I arrived, (and how many joined the group), I was able to sit in the same place—on the left hand side of the settee—facing the fireplace. Little did I know that 'time' was going to be significant factor tonight.

We all had a few minutes to catch up with each other and relax with a quick drink. Robert said an opening prayer, then we chanted the Gayathri Mantra:

> *"Aum Bhur Bhurvah Suvah*
> *Tat Savitur Varenyam*
> *Bhargo Devasya Dheemahi*
> *Dhiyo yonah Prachodayat."*

Resting on the fireplace mantlepiece, was a large ornate gold framed mirror. It perfectly captured the three foot tall picture of Swami (dressed in His saffron robe), which hung directly opposite … on the centre of the wall behind me. His reflection appeared to fill the room and lovingly watch over us. We made ourselves comfortable for the reading.

Lesson: **RHYTHM**

"I hear your heartbeat. Like a drum, it beats to a regular rhythm, which echoes across time, space, and all dimensions. So, you may well ask, if I connect all hearts to mine, how could I possibly hear any one individual soul over the collective thoughts and feelings of billions, and all the elements of life?

Well, know that it is easy, for even though you are more intricate than any fragment of your DNA, you are all unique. Therefore, your soul's divine essence and light resonate to and from me with such simplicity that recognition is instantaneous. It is no more complex than knowing parts of my 'self', as I live within each one of you, remember? So, we are one (as I keep reiterating), and you are never alone no matter if you are held in a vice like grip by your greatest fear … or are enjoying many of the pleasures of living.

As I feel and sense and hear those imaginary lows and highs, please try to treat both with equanimity. This will enable you to treat criticism and praise in the same vain. It will also bring balance through and from your being, which consequently reduces and then eradicates the ego ... which serves only hate, anger, and pain. It would be wise to dispel and remove this as soon as possible.

Indeed, it has no place in the rhythm of life, as will try to deny my working with—and through—you. Only egoism refuses to believe that the 'doer' of your actions can only be for, and from, your 'self'. In relation to this, one should consider your actions are only karmic, which manifests in every avenue ... all walks of life, and in all 'beings'. In fact, you could go as far to say karma is the creator of life, giving cause for many births to the 'earth-plane' throughout the history of one's soul.

Do not misunderstand what you read, hear, or comprehend about this. By now you have grown to realise that no matter what the reasons for one's rebirth to the physical and impermanent world may be, it is love and only love which ultimately sustains and transcends your energy to permanent peace. This is the truest desire, need, and goal of your soul.

So, do you feel you are repeatedly walking or travelling on the same old track, or have you recognized the junction ahead? Are you now ready—and prepared—to make the change(s) to feel fulfilled? And also share the beauty of life and love within you, to all whom you encounter on a new and different course?

Like a signal, I have always given you the green light to be whom you were born (and where you need) to be. Therefore, you need to recognize you have had these choices all along, but have previously denied who, what, and why you live and exist.

It is not to satisfy worldly desires, for they only bring further 'attachments'... shackling and restricting you from fulfilling your true self and being. Such things can spiral out of control, and only attempt to divert you away from the path of truth. When one becomes worried, it can lead to stress, disease, or depression ... if left unchecked.

Try to be content by living in the present, then the concerns of the past—and for the future—disappear. This is not a course or route where if one fails to plan, then you plan to fail ... it is quite the opposite! When you regain control of your thoughts, words, and deeds, then the 'right' action prevails. It is only 'goodness', in terms of what is seen, felt, or heard, which ensues ... not just for yourself, but for those around you, too.

Please understand, throughout one's journey, you can eradicate bad karma, just like a poison. Now compare this with the body. At least once in your life you would have been ill, becoming sick in the stomach. In such circumstances, these are the toxins which your body needs to remove, and which cause you to throw up.

In such an instance, you should not take medicine to stop you feeling nausea; it is only afterwards this should be taken. This is because when the negativity and imbalance have been removed, one may feel weak, but then healing can begin. Similarly, with the ego I mentioned earlier, it will cling like poisonous ivy, but in removing it will only strengthen you, and thus lead you onto greater things.

This does not differ from those trials and tribulations you face in various degrees. Many of you perhaps state I must say that you each deserve what you get (which may sound harsh), but it is down to you, the individual, to either accept or deny what you feel within your own heart. Remember, only you can question the validity and 'experience' of such.

It is the same with disagreements and arguments; anger is not transferred when one stays calm, and replies are given in whispers. You cannot work the flame of ego into a frenzy. This gives the one who remains within equanimity the true power, and also peace; indeed, it is a heavenly peace. The contaminants of hate, frustration, and fear are not digested within the mind.

Therefore, further imbalance is not taken on board. If one remains doubtful of such, then simply try this when a disagreement (in its various layers and forms) lands upon your door. This is not a game but living within the true rhythmic state and energy of love.

Which brings me back full circle, and once more to our eternal connection. So, throughout the Universe you can hear me, and the frequencies of light and sound which scientists track with radio waves are no more than all of what we are: 'Creation.'

Indeed, people continually state there must be life 'out there', or totally assume otherwise; by thinking they can only find intelligent life upon the Earth. However, there are countless planets and beings, more than the stars you bear witness to in the night sky. Currently, humankind cannot 'see' the whole truth, or beyond the dimension of time and space in which you all live. So, to fully appreciate and understand the marvel of it all, then one must first turn within. It is the only way.

Therefore, when you connect with me in your heart, the truth becomes known. In seeing and believing you are a spark of divinity; it is easier to comprehend that a soul is the real 'star'. As such, the answers are all inside every one of you. Amen."

Silence befell the group, and with a soft chime of the bell the meditation started. All of a sudden, it was as if Sai floated out of the mirror to stand in the centre of the room! His crown of hair represented each of us as a thread, entwined together ...linked and fixed upon His heart and soul. His hair began to spiral around the room, and then above us, like a thick mattress cushioning us from any mental instability. Our worries and fears shall not penetrate or disturb us here. This was His protection ... His 'protein' ... energy and oneness. Baba stood before each of the group and seemingly peered into our hearts.

Issy: I noticed the hands of a clock face materialise in front of her. "The hands of time are constant like our love. Memories can fade for every human being, but truth inside your heart and the connection to mine is eternal. People can forget each other in so many ways ... but I will not forget you and your soul."

Manny: "Your life's path and journey may swing like a pendulum in a grandfather clock ... back and forth, back and forth. But one day, your destiny will be to remove yourself from the cycle of death and rebirth into everlasting bliss. This is my promise to you, so just believe in love and truth."

Jan: "My child of light who illuminates the path for others to see. People think of time, or the right time to do this and that. Trust in me is all you need to do. I know what you need and when and why. Listen to the clock of our hearts, combined as one always."

Keith: "Let music be the food of love. The perfect cord is the one that connects your heart to mine. It resonates and beats to perfect rhythm, and our love reverberates throughout the eons of time. Your soul is an everlasting echo of my joy and peace."

Kimmy: "Your light is a symbol which illuminates through the shadows and sands of time. Where doubt and fear raise their ugly heads, you will continue to shine and attract those who need assistance. Therein, people will understand the truth and be guided upon the road and path to find the reality of peace and love."

Kate: "Each second, minute, hour, day, week and year of life can be a moment whereby you learn and grow, but also share the truth and light from within. You are never alone ... I am inside, outside, above, and below you. Follow your heart, always … and you will be following me and yourself as 'one'."

Julie: "Regarding 'time', have a pregnant pause with me … or rather, a birthing of new knowledge and wisdom awaits you. Your inner child has been nurtured and will now reveal the glory of love–and me–to all who open their hearts."

Robert: "Life is like an egg timer, but do not ever worry about time elapsing, or running out. The grains of love and truth filter through one side to the other—eternally. Life is for love … forever, in its many forms and appearances. Ther seeds are sown and your soul's growth and destiny continue unabated."

I went to place my pen down. I glimpsed a smile upon Swami's face, as His presence began to fade … exactly when the soft chime of Roberts table bell, announced the end of the meditation. Wow! Circle:

"Lokah Samastah Sukhino Bhavantu,
Lokah Samastah Sukhino Bhavantu,
Lokah Samastah Sukhino Bhavantu

Shanti, Shanti, Shanti!

After the absent healing and prayers and salutations, and partaking of Vibhuti, each devotee held the feather, sharing their own meditation experiences, before I read Baba's guidance with everyone. A lovely cup of tea and light snacks followed. A 'one-derful' evening indeed! Thank you for your presence and grace, beloved Sai. Praise be to God. Om Sai Ram … Amen."

Although this particular transcript of Swami's guidance, comes from the Circle/meeting at Easter, 2017 … I actually received the 'lesson', just after Swami had left His mortal coil, in 2011. The relationship between them is very interesting. On one hand (before His passing), he compares a merry-go-round with the cycle of birth and death … but then utilises similar symbolism, to educate and inspire and display His love upon each member of the group. I recall the joyous scenes, from the meditation experience, as if they were yesterday.

Spring had arrived, and with it, a sense of optimism and gratitude for the lighter nights, and of warmer days to come. There's nothing like a blue sky and some sunshine to give us all a lift. I know we should appreciate every season, but I'm definitely someone who is drawn to that big, golden ball, above!

Everyone had arrived in plenty of time for the Circle, which meant we were able to chat for longer. Robert had made some early drinks, which we enjoyed. There was a lovely feeling of unity, peace and harmony within the group. It was always good to share positive vibes, and encourage each other in our lives. As we settled down, and became still for our opening prayers, it just seemed that something special would take place this evening. We began with the mantra as usual:

> ***"Aum Bhur Bhurvah Suvah***
> ***Tat Savitur Varenyam***
> ***Bhargo Devasya Dheemahi***
> ***Dhiyo yonah Prachodayat."***

I paused for a moment, then shared an emotional reading/transcript—which I had received after the devastating news, that Swami's 'body' had died. It felt that God was speaking to me …through me, as if to console my heart, and return joy to the forefront of my mind, which could then be shared to uplift every devotee around the world, and beyond.

Lesson: **RE-UNION**

"To all who open their hearts, minds, and souls ... welcome, welcome, welcome! Now then, imagine you are sitting in a garden. The sun is glowing, and as a breeze flows through the branches of the trees, their leaves weave and dance upon my breath, which seems to call and make you aware of my presence.

Please understand, I wish to lift thy heart, elevating your love to new heights for you to experience and share both peace and bliss. And, even though the title above implies a re-connection—which can create false symbolism inside the mind—in truth ... what we write today confirms and brings recognition to the hearts of many.

For millions of people across the world right now, in particular those with a Christian faith—as well as those devotees of Sai Baba—these last few days bring emotions to the surface. However, even despair and anguish can lead to the acknowledgement of truth, and an elation of amazement and realization. During such times, people wonder how a complex array of thoughts and feelings manifest and influence one's heart, by not only shedding tears of fear and sadness, but wonderful joy, too.

Realise too, through eras of old and these so-called 'modern' years, each faith can inspire one and the many. For instance, the Easter period renews thoughts over the resurrection of Christ—which was a victory over death of the body—and the miracle of being 'one' with me. Likewise, with Sai, the Avatar of your current age, who departed his physical body on Easter Sunday morning was not by chance, but as a reminder to everyone of this auspicious time.

Remember, you are not a body with a soul, but you are a soul who wears the body like an overcoat or vessel, which enables experience and emotions to materialize as an expression of me. You could call this a union, a partnership, or a blessing, but only when the physical is discarded, does the important re-union takes place.

Some find this controversial, particularly when a soul undertakes a short sojourn—soul-journey—into the impermanent world, such as a new-born baby or young child. With this notion, do not be disturbed, confused, or cry out with anger or frustration, because you are all divine … and therefore, made your own karmic choices prior to embodiment.

Life is a lesson for the individual and their next of kin, as well as connections further afield, too … like twigs at the end of a large branch on a tree. All are connected in some way, shape, or form. Therefore, cause and effect exist in the relationship between man and all life.

At the time of one's passing, especially those who reach old age, the exterior 'you' becomes weak and brittle through its experience and reduction of energy within the body. Even more so, for those who take on the negativity and the ills of the world, which help to ease the burdens of pain, uncertainty, and fear from humanity. Remember, when the body is spent—resembling a coat with no buttons and holes in the pockets—it cannot insulate or give protection to the internal organs anymore. Like being in a photographer's darkroom, it develops a negative … exposed to more ills than it can bear.

Therefore, I manifest and live amongst you as great teachers, Avatars, and supreme figures of 'Godhead'. Through them, you come to realise the truth. Their brilliance and luminescence could be felt—and seen for miles—such is the power of their love. You should also appreciate that each of you can shine brighter, internally, and externally, right now and every passing day. (These choices, though, are always yours to make).

Throughout history, if people did not witness and experience these miracles of light, the world itself might be so overcome by darkness, hate and greed, you would think it impossible to emerge and live anew. But having done so enables you to bear witness to reality, and I reveal the true image not only for the soul, but to guide many toward their goal, too.

In addition, it does not matter where you live because everyone can grow to understand this through different faiths. This is because they all lead to the religion of love, though their interpretations can dilute, abuse, and confuse, influencing the 'monkey' mind with illusion and confusion. Here, one must appreciate it is not love, which creates anger, conflict, or war.

So, where does this currently leave us? Well, because you are reading or listening to this book, you have already taken much more than baby steps. You are beyond infancy. Like a student, you must decide whether to continue in the school of life, through the re-education of your heart and mind and soul. You comprehend the truth, but 'remembering' it disciplines, transforms, and purifies from within.

Picture yourself peeling an orange. Why does one do this? Surely, you can digest and partake of it whole, can't you? You could, but you do this to reveal the true desire of your palate. Indeed, the sun grows the seed, while the water of life nourished and helped it to mature, and just like the fruit and juice … your light is also the essence, your purpose and goal.

You do not hanker for the orange skin, because you long for the nectar inside. Similarly, when you are ready—on a soul level—you peel away the outer layer (the body), which has hidden the true value and beauty it contains. Resembling a mirror image, I can compare those who desperately need to quench their thirst to the desire to unify and merge into me. Do not be confused, for you are already part of me—as stated many times before—but it is you, as a body and soul, who believes you have become detached from me.

Understand then, when your overcoat has been cast aside, I reveal your divinity in all its glory and splendour … while many friends and family over many generations will have the opportunity to witness and greet you from the false curtain of deceit. Then, while some who loved you on the 'earth-plane' grieve and despair, others (within lighter elements of vibration, experience, and knowledge), know your spark has burst into spirals of light—both beautiful and magical—into happiness, bliss, and peace.

It is important to remember, you cannot purposely remove this yourself, as there are inbuilt safety mechanisms which usually prevent you from self-harming, unless of course … illness of body or mind dissipates the action of truth. In these cases, many lessons are learned both on a soul level, and for the family or friends, who believe it has left them 'behind'.

Through self-realization, you do not need to dispense of the 'body' … like having to peel an orange. By turning 'within' to the stillness, you will find me and feel my love. There you are sustained without the fake glitter and imaginary sparkle, so readily available in the impermanent world around you.

Therefore, do not be sad here, and never fear when I am near. All life is but a click of your fingers. One assumes your experience of 'time' is long, when in fact it is but a whisper upon the wind or can seem like fragments of the imagination. This is why your soul could experience many generations of re-birth and karma.

Finally, I would like you to imagine yourself as the only adult (and person), at a fairground. Would you embark upon a child's ride? Is there a false desire to go around in circles? Is this the moment to come off this pretend playful merry-go-round? Are you now ready to board the express train in the true tunnel of love? No ticket is required ... remember?

Know that you can converse with Sai right now ... just as you have always done."

KEEP ON TRACK ... with SAI BABA

**"Time to then experience, a journey straight and true,
Stuck onto the tracks, with my love, it's just like glue.
No safety belts or fear, when I hold you 'oh so dear',
Those tickets not required, being burdened by your tears."**

So much pain and anguish, but now you're free at last,
Peace and bliss ... our memories ... but they come and go so fast.
I had looked at all your life, what you said and you had done,
In truth your love eternal, has more than just begun.

**"Remember, my words reflect the future, and upon the past,
As you pass beside the body, some stand and stare aghast.
In visions and in dreams, I will remind you of the truth,
My body was a vessel ... to be used for living proof."**

I love you my dear Swami, please remember that is all,
And yes, received your message ... of your Darshan, my one true call.
To continue and to strive, to live through and in the heart,
For we remain as one, forever from the 'start'.

**"So, mourn if you now must, but only for a while,
As the stone was rolled away, for eternally wide smiles.
My cloth it was pure white ... often orange, and next time green,
Deep within your heart, you will know exactly what I mean."**

Yes, your life it was a message, and you tried to say it all,
To come unto your bosom, we waited for your call.
Both the rich and so did poor, came from nations far and wide,
For your omnipotence and omnipresence, as none of us could hide.

**"You may think you're far away, but you're always near and dear,
It is time to stop the crying ... and the shedding of those tears.
For I am always there, as you sit and when you weep,
My hands they hold your heart, and you are safe within my keep."**

Okay I will go, to live in truth ... part of your play,
Yes, be kind tomorrow, and for you SAI every day.
A need of who I am, and what was born to be,
Still walking amongst us all ... beyond eternity.

Amen/Om Sai Ram.

<u>Remember!! Remember the day ... Sung by Ajnish Rai.</u>

(When I listen to this song by Ajnish ... it pierces my heart. And yet, it brings untold joy of our connection with Swami, having experienced His beautiful blessings and peace and grace, within my soul. I hope it resonates inside you, too).

A minute or two passed in silence and the chime of the bell was rung. Once the meditation started, it was if the ceiling of the room disappeared to reveal the night sky above. A celestial celebration as Swami was here! Rainbows, beautiful colours manifesting as party streamers all swirling. It was as if were all magically transported to a universal fairground.

A huge merry-go round with beautiful horses appeared in front of us. We all sat upon them ... it began to speed up ... around and around, we go. Lights and stars sparkled all about us. We dance through the cosmos attached only by His love. Smiles and jubilation abound ... a circle, a ride, carrying ourselves ... for ourselves ... returning to ourselves. Sai's face seemed to glow with happiness, because of our happiness.

Manny: "You ride a grey horse between worlds of Earth and 'Heaven' ... not to return to darkness, but being led to the light. Enjoy this 'ride'. It is free, just like your soul to return home, always, to me."

Jan: "The black horse is only symbolic. Life can seem to be lived in the unknown. What's around the corner are those 'what if's' and 'wherefores', but you are saddled (and seem fixed) only by what the mind thinks is going to happen next. Forget mind. Listen to your heart, and you will always make the right decision. I hold the reins, remember?"

Kimmy: "The purple horse supporting you is in the middle row ... not large or small, but 'medium'. Spiritual awareness of what's around you. Allow the colours to radiate through you to bring guidance and wisdom to those who need it."

Keith: "Your silver horse sparkles like frost upon a moonlit night. Like a crest of a wave, ride it without fear. I am the current who directs you. Do you remember another horse, 'Quick-silver'? Well, my love is the engine on your journey, the horsepower within your soul. And, it is eternal."

Kate: "Your horse, both yellow and gold, glows like the sun. As you ride, it leave a trace like a circle, which lays before and after you ... just like your love. Believe it to be so, for it touches those beyond the four walls in which you reside. Your heart displays the truth, so let others see and know the same."

Robert: "Your steed is white. Clear and pure it resonates with light. Others may not bear witness to the brightness of what lies within and without. Help them to remove rose-coloured glasses, and know that what is in 'I', is in you, is in them too."

Suddenly there are multi-coloured streamers flying in the wind. We all hold on to them ... and we begin to spin around and around like a maypole, drawn in and spun closer and closer to the connection and the love of our own making. We realise that His reins (and reign) guides and protects us on all our journeys.

As Swami's image begins to fade from view, "Understand that as you sow, even nature reaps. We are always one."

Robert rings the small table bell and the meditation ends an incredible experience. Only by Baba's grace could this happen. Prayers and healing and salutations conclude the meeting. Circle:

> ***"Lokah Samastah Sukhino Bhavantu,***
> ***Lokah Samastah Sukhino Bhavantu,***
> ***Lokah Samastah Sukhino Bhavantu***
>
> ***Shanti, Shanti, Shanti!"***

Vibhuti was given to us all by Robert. Kate and Keith served drinks, then everyone went to the dining table for the food they prepared earlier. The devotees each held the feather and discussed what occurred in their own meditations, after which, I shared Baba's guidance and blessings and what had occurred within the Circle. This concluded a truly wonderful and inspirational evening. Thank you beloved Swami ... praise be to God. Om Sai Ram ... Amen."

This next meditation contained wonderful symbolism. And, I was surprised that Sai Geeta, (Swami's elephant), also made an appearance with Baba. Obviously, Swami must have had His reasons why Geeta was there. Usually, it is for the circle's protection, but you could also say that Swami and Sai Geeta, were inseparable. Whenever Sai was away ... apparently she was like a cat on a hot tin roof ... swaying her trunk from side to side, and constantly pacing about. The expression that 'love knows no bounds' is so true!

After a brief catch up with everyone, we all settled down for a few minutes. Calming our bodies, and more importantly, our minds for the meditation to come. Robert led with our usual prayers before the Circle chanted the mantra:

> *"Aum Bhur Bhurvah Suvah*
> *Tat Savitur Varenyam*
> *Bhargo Devasya Dheemahi*
> *Dhiyo yonah Prachodayat."*

Lesson: **HOLLOW**

"Many people continue to yearn and search from outside of themselves. They look towards the exterior world for illumination and meaning, but there will forever be the feeling that something is missing ... like an incomplete jigsaw puzzle.

One may notice such because the picture or scene has a space ... or in the case of one's life, you become unfulfilled, with hopes and dreams falling by the wayside with disappointment or regret. If you currently find yourself, or seem to approach this scenario—no matter what your age, colour, or sex—would you just accept it as 'fate'? Or could you pick yourself up from the floor once more?

What experience of your body, mind, or soul could help you re-ignite the passion of, and for, the truth? How about gazing upon a beautiful sunrise or sunset, or reading or listening to sacred words or poems? Perhaps you can find this spark within a warm smile, or feeling a loving embrace which somehow keeps the flame of love and light ... alight? One only needs to pause and reflect upon the 'wonder' all around you to feel amazed at such peace and beauty. You can find this in colour, texture, shapes, or sounds, which transcends to touch your heart and soul.

If this wasn't the case, perhaps there are those who would call such an individual blind, morbid, depressed ... or worse still, heartless, soul-less, or even hollow. Understand, though, no one would really wish to be viewed or be known this way. In truth, any creature or person (and soul) would resemble a zombie. Others might state they resemble the 'living dead', but in fact, they are neither 'living' nor 'dead', in the true sense of these words.

So, as you make your way through life, are you on 'auto-pilot'? If so, do you really believe that you can live in a vacuum, devoid of truth, love, and happiness? In reality, would such a vacuum exist 'inside' or 'outside' of you? Sadly, in continually blaming oneself, you can get caught in a downward spiral. A forceful sense of desire, fear, hate, or anguish can seem to suck the very life force and energy—the positive aspect of both living and being—from within you.

Every one of you must remember you can be in control of how you feel and react to any situation. By constantly monitoring your thoughts, you can change so much emotionally, physically, mentally, and spiritually, both inside and out. You can, therefore, attract positive energy, goodwill, kindness, generosity, and peace into your life and to the door of your home.

That said, in today's society, one might imagine that they would have to go somewhere to create, change, or even repair some aspect within themselves. But what could need fixing? Does someone need to change their opinions, beliefs, attitudes, or even their looks and appearance to satisfy another? And, with your opinions, feelings, thoughts, hopes, and dreams, can there really be a so-called 'empty' space after all?

Instead, by removing any rose-coloured glasses, you can see with the internal lens of your heart ... which will allow you to witness the truth. You'll know that you are not merely this body, but a soul, residing in a 'vessel'. This enables you to remain in this lower, denser vibration and energy to relearn, and grow. So, when karma has been fulfilled and your life 'complete'—be it for only one second or minute, one hour or day, one month or year, or even three scores and ten—the soul then departs, and the vessel becomes lifeless to the naked eye.

People will often assume that their loved one is still in their arms. They associate memories of their presence with the physical body, but they are now hollow, in the true sense of the word. For all this, they are even closer to them, than can be imagined. The veil—this curtain of deceit called 'death'—is only an illusion, like a mirage.

Some may feel confused by this, implying I even contradict words or meanings. I urge you to feel them inside of you ... and not with the mind.

One's body, becoming 'hollow' through death (and not through a way of living) can be reinterpreted as being 'Holy' or whole. Though—while in your embodiment—it is unfortunately easier to believe in separateness and division, both from each other, and me. With your self-realization, all becomes clear. Selfishness leads to selflessness. Hate turns to love. And through your divine spark, you witness every soul ... just as holy and sacred, as you all are to me.

So, rather than an emptiness, where one lives each day seemingly without purpose, I can fulfil you. You will feel it and know the difference inside and out of your being. Your words, thoughts, and deeds, which were once diverse, and now seemingly 'pigeon-holed' into various components of life—like work, rest, and play and full of desires to please the mind—will change.

Subtly at first, but over time, you will become cognizant of what you're actually thinking. The consequences of such, and what you speak and do, will be kinder and of a more caring nature. These will then flourish, allowing you to nurture relationships with friends, family, kith, and kin in ways of truth. And not from what one can gain, accumulate, or even seek for 'self'.

This pretend 'void' is nothing other than the illusion of doubt which attempts to eat away from within. Left unchecked, it can easily change from nagging doubts or frustrations which lead to anger or hate. Before you know it, they push the goodness and love to one side. It might seem much simpler to forget you ever had it at all, but you have love, are love, and always will be.

Therefore, I ask you to rely on and trust in yourself ... and therefore me. As we are 'one' body, one light, one truth, then you only need to believe. You can do this; you only need to try. Once you do, it is self-perpetuating, because, like a thirst, it will need to be quenched.

Indeed, 'truth' can be searched for in faraway places, upon sacred sites and from many people ... whether they are paupers, presidents, or kings. However, it is in your heart that you will find your true self and me and the truth which is right for your soul. This way, what is usually seen by others (your exterior self, the wrapper and shell), will be replaced by the beautiful radiance and glow of your true essence ... the inside 'out'.

The shining light—which is your reality—will enrich others through your gentle touch, soothing words, and kind gestures. This may surprise those who know you, and more so ... those you don't. in fact, even those strangers who pass through your day and life seemingly unnoticed.

Know that change in any way does not need or have to wait for tomorrow. By truly living for today, tomorrow will take care of itself. This way, the daily seeds you sow will grow and come to bear the fruit of truth with true human kindness. Amen."

After the reading, we all became still within the silence ... and the half-hour meditation began. I could sense the energy beginning to intensify as both Swami and Sai Geeta entered the room! Sai waves to the group, but it is not a hello ... because he has never left us. It is a sign of friendship and love. "Be still, and know the truth of you. We are one ... when all is said and done." He turns to each person and wants me to transcribe his message.

Manny: "Welcome dear child of light. Do not worry about the direction to take, decisions to make. Let your heart be the guide which leads you only on the correct path. Know that I am forever by your side, observing and willing you to live through truth and love. Let the sun and 'Son' shine through your thoughts and words and deeds. Positivity will reign and you will always make the right choice. Do not fear when I am near."

Jan: "Blessed be. I am the blanket of warmth and love. My voice sounds across the ether to let you know I am by your side. Lean on me a helping hand as and when you feel you need extra support in the physical or spiritual realms while you are awake or while you sleep. Understand life is full of unknowns, but love is the one certainty to protect and shine and nurture … and keep your heart alive within me, we are one, remember."

Keith: "Cast your mind back to when you were a small child, recall the sweet melody of a lullaby. Now, as years roll on, allow the musical notes to resonate inside your mind but more importantly your heart. Each one has a different frequency which captivates and then elevate your soul to the higher realms and dimensions. May you ride along the rhythm and beat which echoes across all time and throughout the universe. Let music be the source of love which takes your imagination beyond the beyond."

Kimmy: "Picture an hourglass and within it, the sands of time. As each grain passes through, do not concern yourself of how much, or how little, you think you may or may not have. Something may have triggered thoughts of your own mortality, but why should anyone ever worry when your heart and soul and your love is immortal? There is so much work to be done, and only when God calls for you to come home, will you, or anyone, lave their mortal coil."

Kate: "Continue to embrace nature … and nature will nurture you dear child. Like The four seasons, allow (or moreover) give yourself the space to flourish. You are a spark of creation, so remember to create and express the truth inside you, in whatever way is most enjoyable and comfortable for you to do so. The earth, the sky, the rivers, are all an expression of me ... and you can do the same."

Julie: "The journeys you take lead you only where you need to be ... and when. Left, right or over you go ... there is no need to worry. You may think you carried those (people) to their destinations, but it is I who am the chauffeur of your heart and soul. I will ease your road and those make believe burdens. Place your trust in me, always."

Robert: "People can often play upon one's heartstrings, but in truth, many do not know what they truly want. May your heart be the knowledge and wisdom and encouragement to guide them to the truth. Shine brightly, and allow the light to work through, to, and from you."

Swami and Sai Geeta stayed in the centre of the Circle. Their energy radiated towards us. Sai raised His hand and then said, "Love all ... all love", before both faded into the ether.

Thank you to our beloved Swami and to Sai Geeta too, for all your help and support and protection in our lives.

After absent healing was sent, and closing prayers, we decided to have a drink and nibbles straight away. Then, as we each held the white feather of truth, shared lovely messages from our experiences and from Sai. Another fabulous evening was had by all. Praise be to God. Om Sai Ram/Amen."

Circle:

"Lokah Samastah Sukhino Bhavantu,
Lokah Samastah Sukhino Bhavantu,
Lokah Samastah Sukhino Bhavantu

Shanti, Shanti, Shanti!"

Due to various reasons, there were times where a few of us, actually met at Keith's house. On this occasion it was just Kimmy, Keith, my friend Jill, and myself. Though numbers were small, we were all looking forward to what the evening would bring. Would Swami come and bless us with his presence tonight? For some reason, especially as it was just before Easter, Jesus kept entering my thoughts.

Keith had lit an incense stick, and also a candle on the small table in front of me. I had a glass of water, next to my cup of tea. After an opening prayer and request for protection and guidance, we settled down and chanted the Gayathri Mantra:

"Aum Bhur Bhurvah Suvah
Tat Savitur Varenyam
Bhargo Devasya Dheemahi
Dhiyo yonah Prachodayat."

I then gave a reading of a lesson, which felt is if it had come directly through source/God: **JOY OUT OF DARKNESS**

"The depths of the night, the deep, the abyss, or you could even say hatred, are all names one may use to describe 'negativity' and fear. In contrast, understand there will always be the 'positivity' and light ... bringing balance to all walks of life, both within and upon every planet, dimension of time and space, and in all vibrations (energy), too. Therefore, even in your darkest hour, nothing can deny or erase the glimmer of hope that exists, because nothing can destroy true light and love.

Throughout 'time', people have written or spoken about these facts, but these are often in confusing, over-elaborated text, or even symbolic in nature. However, one must realize the **key** to truth, knowledge, and wisdom is simplicity ... and your 'heart' is the **lock.** Once combined, these reveal a true insight into my love.

Appreciate too; when those soft, musical notes flow around the room in which you sit, they energise and vibrate with immense purity. These are not material or transient to the physical but move in waves of peace towards all who gather, read, or hear these words, and within these moments, no bewildered looks of expression settle here. Even if a soul seems lost, confused, or at the point of giving up ... their spark can still illuminate, so at this Easter time, a special reflection of your faith will mirror in many a heart's flame.

Remember, when Lord Jesus was crucified, the heavens went black. Many believed the world was ending, screaming out, "How could the Saviour die? Why did he not save himself? Why did God not save his Son?" Of course, on the third day, Jesus ascended from the impermanent plane upon the Earth, and hence 'joy came out of the darkness'.

He had indeed endured the most incredible pain, not only from the cross, but also inside his heart by the very people he had come to guide ... and lead back to me. Please comprehend his experience was necessary and ordained by me, acted out by destiny and fate, to guide you all from the depths of shadow and into the light.

In fact, to clear unbalanced karma (and find him), simply enter your true heart, for the Lord sits in the seat of every soul. He is part of the eternal flame of golden love, and his magnificent light emanates and permeates in all directions, flowing in a constant gentle stream, washing and wearing away the rocks of your sin, you yourselves created. This will gradually erode or instantly make it vanish, for purity and truth shine without boundaries, and can conquer all fears and ills.

Please note, sometimes the imbalance resembles granite because of the depths of darkness residing there. In addition, many lifetimes may need to be undertaken for this to be dissolved by the bearer, because many lessons must be learned through themselves, or by—and for—those they live, meet or work with, or even those strangers who pass by in the blink of an eye.

Over time, though, even this turns into dust, similar to your physical bodies, until 'you' become 'balanced' in every sense of the word. Remember though, even dust leaves a trace, and so does the memory of each lifetime and journey, which is your legacy.

This Easter, try to rediscover your inheritance, for the reconnection to bliss may even form part of one's deepest, darkest hour. You only require an open heart, free will, compassion, and forgiveness, but are these all too much? No! For such things are within you all, so please act upon them once they have been recognised 'inside' oneself.

Therein lies the choices you can make, and these are clear for the soul. The Lord did not falter in his quest, goal, and 'work' to bring my love, vision, insight, and light to you all. In recognising the truth upon the cross, you rediscover your own: one light and one love within all ... from all ... and to all.

Once known, the individual must discount and deny, or embrace and accept, who, what, and the why they 'exist'. Remember, when sunshine falls upon your face, you feel uplifted, happy, content ... but when the eternal light radiates and rests inside your heart, you will realise you are already complete.

Imagine the happiness and smiles from distraught parents when they find their lost child, or the stranded are airlifted to safety ... perhaps it is in the discovery a loved one—thought trapped—is actually, alive and well. One may comprehend these scenarios and many more like them, but even these are fragments of elation compared to the feeling of oneness, and the glory of love and light.

So, after fulfilling your life's work and karma and destiny, you will eventually cross over into the permanence of me, which is your 'homecoming'. However, this is not a game or a roll of dice, but is entered voluntarily and willingly by all souls.

Indeed, you have all required 'time' to complete what you need to do, so use this wisely in whatever you wished for (and required) to become the best human being you can be. Release your never-ending supply of my love ... for truth, honesty, compassion, and forgiveness. Be what you all were, are, and always will be ... a part of my expression, shining both peace and joy out of the darkness!"

A SOUL'S GOAL

"You strive to be 'one', yet you are already free,
And your soul is a branch or a leaf on the tree.
To then float upon the breeze and be taken by free-will,
Though sometimes you will struggle, to climb up life's hill.

You journey alone, and yet we are never apart,
While a connection is in truth, if the heart is ajar.
And like a door so strong, made of fine spiritual oak,
Enter and be bathed, by my joy; lie and soak.

Emerge and sustain in your new zest for life,
Be gentle and kind; love your friend, husband, or your wife.
So, walk the good walk and talk the good talk,
And be true to your soul, to fulfil your true 'goal'.

Amen."

Our thirty minutes of silence began.

As soon as the meditation started ... there were dark clouds swirling around the ceiling of the lounge. An eagle came into view, soared high (yet beneath the storm), which I knew was for our protection. Jesus appeared before us, nailed to the cross. My heart gasped, and seemed to miss a beat. Suddenly he came down to meet us, and appeared in the centre of the Circle. His crown of thorns began to illuminate and fill the room with brilliant light. The darkness had been cleansed. "Tonight, I celebrate my love with you. Each thorn bears no pain, but radiates like stars, throughout Creation.

May you each be like a candle flame, glowing brightly in the darkness ... for those less fortunate than yourselves. During lent, one may often give up so-called normal things, but these may be immense issues to another, perhaps they are things that people in faraway places, can only dream of.

So, during these 40 days and 40 nights, may the sweetness and fragrance from the perfume of my heart, now flow through each and every one of you. It is to be given freely and willingly, to those whom you meet or greet. Please understand, all the trials and tribulations are but experiences which provide you with knowledge and wisdom. Therefore, you are each given the opportunity to share these with fellow beings, and souls. May you all emerge stronger, and brighter, as a result. Go and be in peace, always and forever, in my love."

Jill: "I offer you my robe ... for protection and strength and fortitude. May my healing love shine through you. (Lord Jesus then knelt and kissed her feet). And, I anoint you now with holy water. By christening your mind and cleansing your soul, my eternal gift is to help you ... through the days of your life and journey ahead."

Kim: (Jesus knelt before her). "I cleanse your feet to offer purity to those who wish to rise up through your love and light. Where you walk, you are in my footsteps ... and so an internal trace forever remains. A journey of compassion and forgiveness cannot be eroded like footprints in the sands of time, washed away by the ebb and flow of emotional waters of life. So, we remain, as always ... 'one'."

Keith: "Come take a walk with me ...it is time to explore pastures new. Here, you will not taste bittersweet fruits, but will stay within my heart. When you stop and pause and reflect upon me, know that my heart and yours are 'one'. Your life is a spark of my everlasting light. Try then, to illuminate the new path that you tread in the knowledge that I am above, below, without, and within. Indeed, 'you will never walk alone', my son." (Keith is from Liverpool in the UK, so the phrase above is both apt, and significant).

Just before the end of the meditation, Jesus raised His right hand. The scene of the last supper began to expand and fill my mind. He looked around the room, and spoke again. " You are my body ... the bread of life. I am your blood and life-force, which runs through your veins. Know that my strength, is your strength. Amen."

In less than a heartbeat, Jesus's presence (though some say His 'light body'), disappeared. Within a minute or two, the meditation period was over. As we had no table bell to hand, I tapped my small glass of water gently with the edge of a teaspoon, to signify the Circle to draw back within themselves.

Once everyone was grounded and fully aware of their surroundings we took it in turns to share our experiences. I read my transcribed notes last of all, before we closed with another prayer and chanting the Lokah Samastah Mantra:

> *"Lokah Samastah Sukhino Bhavantu,*
> *Lokah Samastah Sukhino Bhavantu,*
> *Lokah Samastah Sukhino Bhavantu*
>
> *Shanti, Shanti, Shanti!"*

We shared some Vibhuti then gave thanks for the Jesus's presence and His beautiful Divine guidance. "Thank you dear heavenly Father/Mother God ... dear Lord Jesus, and beloved Sai too for what we have received by, and through, your grace." Keith brought out some fabulous biscuits with another cup of tea. On the way home I dropped Jill off ... and kept thinking what an incredible evening it was! Om Sai Ram/Amen."

For the second meeting in a row, I met with Keith, Jill and Kimmy at Keith's home. It was about ten minutes to eight in the evening when Jill and I arrived there, so we only had chance for a brief catch up of each other's news. Kimmy had prepared the room, a candle was lit and incense too. After opening prayers of love and protection, we chanted the mantra:

"Aum Bhur Bhurvah Suvah
Tat Savitur Varenyam
Bhargo Devasya Dheemahi
Dhiyo yonah Prachodayat."

I then read the following lesson: **SACRIFICE**

"For many people across the world, a memorable date and time approaches once more. Soon, the eleventh hour on the eleventh day of the eleventh month becomes significant for generations, both past and present. Please understand, it not my intention to make anyone feel sad, frustrated or even unsure of the why, what and the wherefores of those who laid their lives on the line, and in doing so, make the ultimate sacrifice.

Realise too, throughout history and the eras of time, conflicts of both heart and mind have ensued across the globe. Likewise, across and upon many planets, planes of energy, and dimensions, too. Is there a reason for it? Can any one person truly comprehend such things? It is more than likely most of you will find this difficult to do, and therefore it is important these passages of text stick to simple analogies and enable a greater understanding for all. Let's just retrace our steps for a moment.

I appreciate—within your everyday life—you can make compromises and personal sacrifices, often with family, friends, neighbours, employers, and towards strangers. One may also give your own time to support another who is ill, lost, cold, hungry, and thirsty, depressed, suffering pain and anguish through the body, mind, or soul.

Remember, I see everything and all things I am. Therefore, I sense these moments as easily as one who wants to open their eyes in the morning. It is instantaneous and happens without thought or word. Know that deeds from the heart shine like starlight, but only when the action is willingly, wantonly, and purposefully, undertaken.

Of course, the recipient will almost always appreciate the results of the act, but the giver—unless proceeding in truth—will not 'resonate' with such a beautiful vibration and energy. This may not be witnessed by those who live on the 'earth-plane', but is readily seen by the light hierarchy, the elementals, and those residing upon different and higher frequencies, too.

Acts of kindness, when carried out with love, reverberate throughout time. They leave an imprint on hearts and souls. They do not fade like footprints on wet sand, or handprints cast as reminders in clay or cement. No, these will all disappear, even this takes thousands or millions of years, because this is inevitable in the impermanent world.

UNITY OF FAITHS

In these modern times in which you live, your thoughts now focus upon the present wars and conflicts taking place around the world, but not forgetting those who previously fought over the decades and centuries. In fact, many of you carry these concerns. You also worry for those who return injured and scarred—emotionally, physically, and mentally—as well as those souls who left their bodies on land, sea or in the air.

I beg of you to be 'united' in love. Every country, nationality, colour, and creed ... but without your attachment to the body. Please know that when you grieve for the 'departed', tears often fall upon your cheeks and lips. There lies the hardest thing which you need to remind yourself of. It might help to recall the following words, "Do not stand beside my grave and weep, for I am not there, I do not sleep", as they resonate in the ether during all such moments of sadness and grief.

Across the world, I bear witness to all religions and faiths. While some people lay symbols and mementoes in gratitude, others (who believe they are left behind) want them to know they are still loved. Crucifixes, poppies, and wreaths are carefully placed upon statues ... while memories and tears fall onto hallowed turf, which all display their love from, through, and to me, and countless other hearts too.

Please strive to steer yourself away from what you call painful or 'sad' times. Always rejoice in the heart's memory, for you are each a wave of emotion on the ocean of my love. One day, every soul will float upon calmer waters. Here, the turbulence of loneliness or false separation soon becomes erased forever from your hearts.

Do not despair in striving to establish a meaning of it all. The reality is not in faraway lands to which you cannot reach or find. Nor is it withheld through the eons of time by sacred texts or words, which can no longer be deciphered. There is no secret 'secret'. Love is the only answer. It is the key, the door, the way, and the truth. Nothing more and nothing less. If this were not so, you would not even exist.

During such times when souls gather to 'remember' … comprehend that the resonance and trace of light from those who you think are 'lost', shine through and to and from and below and above you. They are also sparks of divinity and love. Therefore, they sense and know your hearts, too.

So, memories of their embodiment and time together with family, friends, and colleagues are as fresh as dew on grass. Their physical bodies may have withered and faded, just like a rose or flower bud—long since picked from its bed—grown upon Earth and nurtured by both the Sun and 'Son'. However, their fragrance, essence and sweetness lie forever safe in my heart … and therefore remain in yours too.

Strange though it seems, time is a great healer. Those who bear a recent passing may deny this, of course. Is this an initial or a natural cause and effect you wonder? Well, just do not fear. Though your mind and memories can indeed fade, your love cannot. It does not matter how or where or when the garment and overcoat of the soul—which you call the body—becomes erased, whether by burial, flame or by any other means.

Therefore, realise there is so much strength within you. Whatever reason, that you cannot be 'still' to find it … then seek it inside others, because their hearts and arms will cradle you as if they are my very own.

Let me take you back for a moment, to a previous 'lesson' of this book. Remember, I explained that by celebrating one's own birthday, it becomes a constant reminder of your embodiment in the world. Well, I am no 'party pooper', but restate this for two reasons.

First, to help you strive from the notion of being body first and soul second—and to lose this attachment inside your minds. Still, those 'gatherings' bring you together as one—even if they are just family and friends—as this brings goodness and confirms connections of hearts. But try to understand the reason behind this, which needs simplifying.

Second, like a birthday, the date of one's passing can also be seen as an anniversary … one which often carries dread, fear, anguish, or anger. Please refrain from these emotions. Only when the physical passes away can the celebration of a life be truly made because the soul has returned once more to their true resonance of being. Remember, they are not within my peace and bliss because I took—or now keep—them away from you, for all things are part of experience, karma, and the light of all creation.

Likewise, those who 'pass over' are as close to you as you want and need them to be. Time, distance, dimension, and different energy and levels cannot detract from the truth that we are all inseparable and are united for all eternity. Therefore, please be glad for each second with those you love and care for. Those cherished times ring and sing like musical notes floating in the ether … falling upon all hearts, minds, and souls throughout my kingdom. Rejoice in your connection and their love, for this can never be erased.

Such understanding is sacred and just, and a sacrifice made in any capacity is righteous and wonderful to sense and witness. In fact, to give one's life to save another is beyond being golden as it becomes a jewel which adorns my crown … and forever glows eternally within both my heart and theirs as one.

Finally, today, please appreciate and acknowledge what one could call the greatest sacrifice known to man … when Jesus gave up his body. This was to remind you of your own divinity—to help you understand the truth—that it is 'within' that you are the true image of me. Amen."

After a few deep breaths, exhaling any negativity and breathing in positive love and light energy, we were now still … and ready, for the spiritual work ahead.

As the meditation started, I am looking into a mirror. I see outlines of two people, one wearing a saffron robe, and the other brilliant white. I knew it was Sai Baba and Jesus, who were drawing close to us. On this occasion, Swami stayed on the peripheral of my vision, while Jesus appeared to float forward. Bizarrely, His image was blurred at first, and then became clearer. It was if I had been gazing into a mirage, like a heat haze over a desert. (This was no '*maya*' or illusion … whereby one believes they are seeing the unreal as real … mistaking the transient for the eternal).

Jesus was concluding his forty days and forty nights of fasting. He appeared to be carrying a pole, with a small bag attached to the end. "These are all your worldly cares and burdens. I will carry them for you all, to bring contentment to your hearts, and clarity to the mind. Know that my love is in your hands and heart, so even in the wilderness, you are never alone. I am your strength when temptations are close at hand. I will lead you all … into the everlasting light. Please come … walk with me." He gazed upon us … and when He spoke, His words were like lullabies … soft and gentle, which soothed and resonated inside us.

Jill: "See me in all things, the sun, the clouds, the trees. Hear me in bird song, the wind, and the leaves that blow around your feet. Feel me with the sunshine on your face, the arm around your shoulder, and the stillness within your heart."

Keith: "Talk the talk and walk the walk, and do what you feel and feel what you do. Look and listen and learn through the lessons of your life. I will carry you through testing times and situations ... so too, with love, you can do the same for others."

Kimmy: "Step forward from another's shadow and emerge as you always intended to be. Let my gifts flow from and through and to you ... so that others may see and feel and know the light as 'one'. No separation or division between souls. You are all the same to me, divine. Let the same divinity be expressed towards others, so that they may find me ... through you, as one too."

Jesus asked us to stop walking, and stay behind. He proceeded ahead of us for about ten seconds, then turned around to face us. He held out His right hand, as if to wave goodbye, yet He spoke again...

"Over hills or valleys, across seas or mountains,
Through air, fire, water and earth ... help the meek, the mild, and the mirth.

Now follow your heart through thick and thin,
No need to scream or shout or make a din.

All hearts are known wherever they may be,
As all form parts ... of the tree of life and 'me'.

So, seek and you will all find ...
True love and light, not for sin or crime.

And the treasure within ... more priceless than jewels or gold,
Is the truth you have heard, and is forever foretold."

Jesus began to fade from view ... as if into a beautiful sunset. Yet this was Swami and Jesus simply merging into one. The sky reminded me of Sai's crown of hair ... with a halo of colours representing his robes he wore on different occasions through the year

... saffron/orange, red, yellow and white. I felt very emotional. Strangely, my soul was blissful ... though my heart ached, because they no longer seemed within my arms reach ... which of course, I know, is nonsense.

I clinked the glass with the teaspoon, and the half an hour meditation had ended. I think it was nearly five minutes before we all became centred once more. Jill, Keith and Kimmy shared their experiences with a small dove's feather, and I followed with the transcribed notes. We all felt so much gratitude for both Sia and Jesus to bless us with their presence in the Circle tonight. It was incredible ... truly 'one-derful'!

We closed the meeting with a prayer and absent healing followed by the mantra:

> *"Lokah Samastah Sukhino Bhavantu,*
> *Lokah Samastah Sukhino Bhavantu,*
> *Lokah Samastah Sukhino Bhavantu*
>
> *Shanti, Shanti, Shanti!"*

After partaking in Vibhuti, we concluded the Cicrlce/evening's joyful work. Keith made some tea and coffees, and we devoured some biscuits. We headed home with happy hearts, peaceful minds, and blissful souls. Thank you dear God, beloved Swami and Jesus ... for your love and protection and guidance, always. "Om Sai Ram/Amen."

Once more, tonight's Circle was to take place at Keiths house. I picked Jill up from her home and set off, eagerly anticipating the guidance we all hoped to receive. After our hello's with Kimmy and Keith, and welcome drinks of tea, we settle down to become still ... away from the hustle and bustle of our day. A candle and incense stick was lit, then we each sent absent healing, and offered our humble prayers for protection and guidance during the meditation. After this, we chanted the Gayathri Mantra:

"Aum Bhur Bhurvah Suvah
Tat Savitur Varenyam
Bhargo Devasya Dheemahi
Dhiyo yonah Prachodayat."

Followed by reading the Lesson: **SURROUNDINGS**

"As always, I welcome you to the connection of our hearts as one. May peace now descend upon all those who bear witness, sense, or feel this upon the planes and dimensions of time and energy and space. Please understand, it is in every soul's nature to desire it above all things. Within peace, the tranquillity and bliss of love sustains all elements of life.

I constantly hear, "Dear Lord, dear Sai (or God), I want peace". So, let me remind you all ... that by eradicating the ego—which is the 'I'—and removing the false desire of the senses (which is your 'want'), you cannot fail to find, or receive, and be left with the peace that is both required and needed.

Some will still ask, "But where is it?" Or, "How can I find this peace?" Well, many people will feel influenced by their surroundings. This often leads to thoughts of where they are born—or now live—which could somehow affect such things. Indeed, perhaps one would find it easier to sense and become peaceful if you could hear birdsong, feel sunshine upon your skin, or see fields of green pastures ... maybe a beautiful shoreline, large hills or valleys and mountains?

You may not be in this position, even preferring to be surrounded by the hustle and bustle of a town or city ... those concrete jungles where brick and stone rise and tower overhead. Of course, some hearts 'like' this feeling, for they somehow seem protected within the shadows cast by the sun. Others not at all, for they can feel disconnected from nature and even from life itself. Everyone has opinions of what seems right or wrong in this respect.

Obviously, by living in built-up areas, those who wish to gaze upon the stars at night cannot see them. The glow and illumination from manmade light—emitted from streetlamps, office tower blocks, factories and many other buildings—will cause a halo of haze which blocks out natural beauty from above, and all around you.

Now then, it is important that you understand I am not stating anyone should suddenly vacate, up sticks, and camp out in the hills, because these comparisons are not—in truth—what this lesson is about. The reason I state these things is to explain that you each make the choice of where, what, why, and how you live your life. Even more than this, that you can make your way to the one place where you can comprehend, experience, grow, and know immense beauty and wonderful things by going nowhere!

In fact, there is no material outlay, and no need to cross a palm with notes or coins from any land upon the Earth. Many will comprehend this, already realising I am referring to the connection within their own heart. This place—through the doorway of love—does not need a key. Nor do you need a special password, or any offering to enter. It makes no difference where you physically live or now find yourself at this time.

It is here and here alone within the stillness that noise and distractions of your surroundings, be it any concern, stress, anxiety, fear, or even the walls and barriers which pretend to segregate you from me, will disappear. Time, space, and all the fabric and materials known and unknown to humanity cannot ever divide or separate us, for we are one and whole.

In such times, comprehend, too, that you are already free. You truly are. Those dividing lines erected through different languages and colours of skin are false. They are formed by the illusion and confusion, cast out by those who believe they can manipulate both body and soul … when they can't.

Remember, throughout history, bodies of many enlightened hearts may have been broken, but the divine essence and spark of love is immeasurable, unique, and eternal. It cannot be cut down by sword or tongue. Nor can it be burnt, buried, or dissolved; it is the only thing which is permanent and everlasting.

So, how do you feel about these words? Do you believe them? If not, could you? Appreciate that you must follow your own truth within yourself. This will lead you to gain wisdom through knowledge and your own life experiences.

This way, every book of text, each person, sage, guru, aspirant, and devotee of truth, can only be deemed as guides. Indeed, they may appear to influence your choices and decisions, but ultimately, it is you and you alone who must decide what resonates inside. You will know what feels comfortable, like your favourite pair of well-worn shoes, which are a perfect fit and seem so right, just as I have often described before.

Take or heed whatever connects with you from this lesson. Perhaps discarding the rest until another page—or day—flows freely inside your heart once more. There is a time for everything. I waste nothing. Therefore, situations and circumstances often repeat themselves in and around you, not to annoy or make one feel upset or desperate, but to show you the way forward. This strengthens you to cope with life's perceived challenges and tests.

For those of later years—especially the retired who have many 'life' experiences—they should be respected. They possess knowledge and wisdom gained through (and from) their periods of work, rest, and play … as well as their joy, grief, love, hate, and any fear. Understanding and peace can then be shared, bringing transition, and understanding to the many.

The state often neglects the elderly. Even family or friends may consider them as a burden, but they can become—and should be—revered by every nation. Please comprehend the old and wise, for they are all part of your own 'being', which in turn forms an integral part of society. Therefore, youth and old age should never be deemed as separate, or divided by spans of time, as everyone has their part to play.

Okay then, where do you go from here? Well, you could think about who, what, and why you are who you are. For all that's said and done, there is a role to play and one for you to fulfil. Also, please try not to merge into the background of your 'surroundings'. In doing so, you are like a chameleon—which changes colour through anguish or fear—actually disguising yourself, trying to remain anonymous amongst your kith and kin.

Know too, that I do not chastise you. Nor do I expect anyone to desire material accolades or medals and awards, but urge and wish for you to strive for the greatest prize of all, self-realization into bliss and peace. Through kindness, right conduct, truth, and love, your divine essence, and spark of true creation within, can once more shine like a beacon. You can become a standard bearer and torch carried aloft, like an Olympic flame, which announces the arrival and coming together of all people as one.

This is not a competition between you all, to see who comes 'first'. By the union of souls, each one of you will stay on the right track together. Appreciate that the events of your lives can then become the fields of dreams, encouraging carrying you forward into eternity.

By setting aside the differences in where each of you live, comprehension of the 'one community' prevails. Indeed, as countless people are going through pain and upheaval—from the immense changes within nations and across continents far away from your own—they may still, one day, touch your own shoreline. If not physically … then mentally and emotionally.

The surroundings where you live may currently appear vastly different. That said, the connection of both joy and suffering knows no distance or time to the heart. So, you can never feel alone or isolated from me, even if one somehow denies or hides away from your fellow man.

No … you may all be a living, burning flame of light, but every single one of you are the plumes of my heart. Together, we are whole. So, whether you're living in a mansion, a slum, even a tent or a palace, these material surroundings are impermanent and transitional. Only when you realise that you're forever surrounded by my love and grace will the permanence of truth be retained … eternally resting within your heart. Amen."

I signalled for the thirty minutes of peace and bliss to begin …with the gentle tap of the tea spoon on a glass of water.

Almost immediately, a ball of gold and orange light descends into the room ... Swami is here! There is a shape within the light which resembles a gyroscope, full of power, spiralling with love. I can sense Sai describing how, 'we are all sparks of Creation'. Light beams flow to each of our hearts, for we are all one and whole. These rays are pulses of energy. They vibrate at different frequencies, each unique and expanding, yet staying linked through thought and word and deed. They seem to tickle my face. Swami speaks, "Just like Mother Nature, everything is connected, to share and support each living thing. Peace and love will reign (and rain) upon all life." Different colours begin to emanate from within the light sphere of love that is Sai ... which flow towards us.

Jill: Blue, for healing. "Remember, you are a wave upon the ocean of my love. Memories can come and go, like the ebb and flow of a tide ... but our love is the constant that cannot ever fade. Each day, take as it comes, in the knowledge that all is as it's meant to be. Trust in me ... trust in yourself, and all will be well."

Keith: "Aah, green for you my 'son' ... for you know what I mean. By removing all ego, and envy, one's true contentment will shine through for others to experience the real 'you'. This, in turn, enables others to learn for their own growth ... and their love can sprout in new directions, too."

Kimmy: Orange. This energy is for assimilation ... merging into the consciousness and pool of your own divine essence. Like the burning sun, may your flame shine eternal, and radiate through time and space. This will help to illuminate the darkness and make the unknown, known ... to those who fail to see, and those who have yet to open their hearts to whom, what, and why they are 'light'."

Baba seemed to drift from my view, though a feeling of tremendous tranquillity and peace descended upon and stayed with me. I was reaching for the teaspoon and glass, as the thirty minutes was almost over, when Swami appeared before us. Once more, He blessed us with His teaching... "All are upon the stage of life. So, always try to give your best performance with (and through), the heart and soul and mind. Every element of life are instruments of my love. If you each shine, you instrumentally love each other. Then, all will realize and understand the same truth within each and every one of you. Amen."

Words cannot begin to describe how wonderful it was to receive Sai's presence this evening. His mercy and grace and love know no bounds. I am truly blessed to be His devotee and scribe for this continuing Circle of trust and hope and friendship.

We shared each other's experiences from the meditation then closed tonight's meeting with prayers, and gratitude. We asked for healing for all life that is suffering, whether mentally, emotionally or in the physical ... followed by chanting the mantra:

"Lokah Samastah Sukhino Bhavantu,
Lokah Samastah Sukhino Bhavantu,
Lokah Samastah Sukhino Bhavantu

Shanti, Shanti, Shanti!"

After partaking in Vibhuti, I helped to make the tea with Keith. His favourite chocolate hobnob biscuits were gratefully received (though they didn't last long ha ha), before saying our goodbye's. Praise be to God, indeed. Om Sai Ram/Amen!

Wow ... in tonight's Circle there were ten devotees present, so it was fortunate that we all arrived in plenty of time. We were able to have a drink before the meeting got underway ... thank heavens for Rob and Kate's coffee and tea supplies! We settled ourselves down, got comfortable, and become focused on the spiritual work ahead. Rob said a prayer of protection and for divine guidance. Before reading a lesson, we all chanted the mantra:

> *"Aum Bhur Bhurvah Suvah*
> *Tat Savitur Varenyam*
> *Bhargo Devasya Dheemahi*
> *Dhiyo yonah Prachodayat."*

Lesson: **FEELINGS**

"Welcome once again. Do not fret about tiredness and the responsibilities of your day, for I will strengthen and empower you to overcome any negative thoughts which may emerge. By being still, you will feel at one with yourself and me, and thereby become focused upon the work at hand.

I urge you to do this, because your conscious and unconscious mind can often hold you in a spell or trick you into believing you are not progressing in some way. Many people think like this, and assume they are not achieving their goal(s), but please do not be too hard upon yourselves.

Over time, the ability to shine your light and love can be measured by how you feel when you are revealing the true inner you. This will become easier by talking calmly and with honesty, so even if your words or a particular moment seem to come through compassion and mercy, or via resentment and hate, truth must always prevail.

Through uncertainty, people often wonder if it is ever right to display anger. Well, this type of energy is only another reflection of 'self', but it limits, restricts, and holds one in a negative state. In fact, you could replace the word anger with 'anchor', and hence, within heated moments, the real questions should be, "How can I rectify what I have said or done, causing you to be so angry with me?" Or, "What is that hurts you so much, that you feel you need to hurt me in order to heal your wound?"

Do not imagine or think this as strange, because when you accept you are all 'one', no division or separation can occur, and you will realise the so-called 'good or bad' merge in everything. In addition, within most daily acts of your life, you will interact with people who irritate and annoy, or are rude and discourteous towards yourself or others. These harmful situations can intimidate with apparent ease, so if your mind switches to a blame scenario, it would be prudent to rise above this.

It would also be wise not to search and mull over any failings of another, but simply overlook them and do not judge. Offer kindness from your heart, which will reflect and magnify their own light, piercing the shadow or cloud lingering over them. Perhaps it is even easier to remember these words … forget the harm others do to you and forget the good you do for another too.

This might seem a hard thing to do, especially when someone suppresses their true feelings, through fear and self-denial, or in case of offending others. There is a fine balance here, and it requires contemplation, because within clarity of thought lays the truth, which enables you to proceed with dignity as a person and soul with true human values.

Remember, people can act strangely, or at least out of character … their behaviour become weird or even bizarre, but why is this so?

Well, there are many reasons to explain this, but most come from stress or 'dis-ease' because of internal pressure upon the body or mind, which can surface in a variety of ways and forms, and sometimes they just snap.

Two important issues are raised here, one being how the person is conducting themselves towards you or others, and second, your reaction ... the effect following the cause. It is true the feelings and emotions displayed by another could have a large impact on the resulting consequences, but they will influence all events and their outcome—for better or worse—depending upon the wisdom of those around them at that time.

Know that you can make a hateful or spiteful situation turn around; with a smile, a whispered word, or by simply offering a helping hand of love and peace. This is the choice only an individual alone can make.

So, how do you feel at this point in your life? Are you bitter, annoyed, confused, and perplexed, or live with a heart that blooms and radiates love, feeling contented, blessed, happy and fulfilled? What does it take for you to become the latter? And do you need to alter something inside yourself? Indeed, it's easy to change your partner, your job or home, but these are all external ... it is the interior you which can be renewed with hope and faith.

Therefore, always believe in yourself, for I promise you, if you have confidence in yourself, you will never look back. Do not doubt the love and light within you, as my grace forever flows over all life, from the tiniest creature or flower, to all beings, throughout creation. Is it favoured or rationed? No, but some imagine or believe I do this, so please look deep into your heart, because inside you will know me ... and find your own truth and self too.

Your belief in me shows up within your 'make-up' too, ranging from your personality and demeanour to the very spark of your life, and therefore how you feel about yourself is also a reflection of me too. Whether you receive praise or condemnation, whether you are rich or poor, clothed or naked, these are all thoughts and elements of the exterior.

To put this in perspective, picture a circle inside your mind. What do you currently think of? Is there anything within it? Or, if you were to consider I am the circle itself, would you believe you were outside of me, and hence unattainable? Do you also deem yourself to be distant in other situations of your life? If so, I implore you to take control of your life and believe with all you are; for you can achieve the true goal of ascension and liberation!

Misinterpret nothing I have said, for I only want you to be happy. Real happiness cannot be found inside the impermanent or physical world. The mind ill continually tempts and trick you with desire. Therefore, you can only 'sense' this when you turn within. There is no other way.

For example, when two people fall in love, they do not worry about what others think or say, because a special feeling makes their whole life flow. They are within themselves and the moment, which captivates, sustains, and fulfils them. True love makes any separation feel unbearable.

However, even though we are all one, and with millions of souls projecting this feeling towards me, millions more still distance themselves from me, and if my heart were physical, it would surely break. Do not fear, though, as I encompass all life and I know each outcome, situation, thought and feeling of every soul and being.

I am light and love; I am all power and all of Creation. Hence, it should be easier to realise I am also your breath and heartbeat, so when you feel the way you do, I do too. Therefore, when you talk, walk, work, rest, or play, express your true feelings so others can share theirs. When your thoughts, words, and deeds are given, every consequence will become mine. Do not worry, for I am within, without, above, below, in front, and behind you. As I have stated many times, you are never alone, for I love you with all that I am.

In your past and present and future, your feelings leave traces of whom and what you are and can become. The tears of truth will fall from eyes and hearts until all souls know we are forever 'one' ... and are simply sparks of the same living, burning, and eternal flame. Amen."

Rob rang the table bell once ... the signal for the meditation to begin. The silence was beautiful. With ten circle members present, the energy in the room was incredible. Sia, wearing his saffron robe, appeared in front of the fireplace ... and Sai Geeta stood tall by his side, providing protection for us all. (When I've been blessed to see Her presence with Sai, it was as if she displayed human emotions. In fact, it has been said that she possessed superhuman, divine traits too.) Baba smiled, as if expressing His happiness with our attendance.

He waved His right arm in a circle and was conveying on a subtle level that love flows from (and through) the universe/Creation ... back to love. "The circle of life, all are 'one'. I celebrate your oneness, every day. Welcome, once more to you all."

Sai looks up. It appears the roof of the house has disappeared and the boundless cosmos floats above us. He raises His hand, which seems to stretch forth into the ether like a rubber band, to plucks stars from the Heavens which now rest between his fingers. He looks at the group and says, "Like you ... diamonds, are forever." There is a sudden and massive shift in vibrational energy. Colours so vibrant and pure, pour outwards from Sai's crown of hair ...which then radiate to each of us in turn.

Martin: White. May the seeker of truth within you, guide you through the peaks and troughs of life. Trust your inner voice ... at all times. " (White is 'all-knowing').

Linda: Indigo. "Inside, your love blooms. Its sweet fragrance I will cast upon the wind of my breath. Honesty and integrity are key witnesses, always."

Kimmy: Blue. As above, so below. Into the blue, but not cold emotions. Seeing with greater clarity ... the eye of body and soul and mind, a gift bestowed."

Julie: Purple: Spiritual gifts for greater insight, revealing the love and wisdom in and through the veil of shadow. New energy is bestowed to learn and grow."

Jan: Orange. "You are my child, no matter what age, or where, you reside. Fostering is a human term, taking another into one's heart. Sharing and providing leaves an eternal trace of gratitude and kindness ... acts never forgotten by our one true heart."

Manny: Red. "I energise you. The core of your own divine spark shall illuminate the pathway ahead. Stay on course and lead others into perpetual light and love."

Robert: Green. "I am forever with thee and shower you with healing and blessings ... for continued strength to grow an share our love within. Allow it shine throughout night and day, into and beyond Earthly vibrations."

Kate: Yellow. "Shine, shine, shine. You are part of the golden sun (and Son), a ray of hope for those who may have lost their way. Truth will guide you ... helping you to help those who struggle to see the light. Be a beacon and draw others through your heart."

Keith: Violet. "Peaceful, softly and radiant ... gently nudging those who become misguided through life's needs. Simple words will flow to uncomplicate life's issues of those who enter and walk beside you on this journey. Enjoy ... as I am forever a companion, and beyond the physical too."

As if right on cue, the bell chimed. Swami waved His hand in a circle ... and He and Sai Geeta disappeared into a vortex of energy ... rising into the cosmos, which then closed instantaneously. I will always be amazed at Sai's love and blessings for everyone. It is beautiful, an honour and a privilege beyond compare.

Robrt closed the meditation with a prayer. We gave absent healing then all chanted the Lokah Samastah mantra:

> *"Lokah Samastah Sukhino Bhavantu,*
> *Lokah Samastah Sukhino Bhavantu,*
> *Lokah Samastah Sukhino Bhavantu*
>
> *Shanti, Shanti, Shanti!"*

Robert gave us all some Vibhuti. Each devotee shared their experiences while holding the white feather. I then shared Sai's divine guidance with the Circle, before Robert and Kate served drinks and some welcome snacks. Phew ... what an evening! We owe so much to Baba and Sai Geeta. Thank you beloved Swami! Om Sai Ram/ Amen. I must have been floating on air driving home, as it went so quickly and smoothly. Praise be to God in then highest.

In this next Circle, at Roberts and Kate's, we nearly had a full house. Wow, ten devotees! It was always wonderful to have balanced numbers, too. You could sense the resonance of energy that built up within the room, especially with five males and five females present.

We had a brief catch up of each other's news, over a quick drink. Then, as it was nearly eight o'clock, we all settled comfortably in our positions. Robert gave an introductory prayer for guidance and protection, and as usual, we chanted the important Gayathri Mantra:

> *"Aum Bhur Bhurvah Suvah*
> *Tat Savitur Varenyam*
> *Bhargo Devasya Dheemahi*
> *Dhiyo yonah Prachodayat."*

I then read a Lesson: **SIGNS**

"Welcome to one and all ... and even though the 'body' may be tired, let your heart be willing to listen, hear, and feel my love. Please understand, throughout time and history, millions of souls have searched day and night for the light. Some climb mountains, believing they become nearer to 'God', while others cross vast seas or sail upon rivers of water and emotion in their attempt to find me. In contrast, there are those who just know the truth, and do not even need to close their eyes in order to sense or 'realise' me.

It is strange that so many of you try to discover who, what, and where I am in these different ways. On occasions, desire can make the 'seeker' believe I resemble buried treasure, and by digging around, they will somehow find the answers to their prayers. Do not mistake me, for I will never belittle or chastise anyone. I urge you all to search with honesty and endeavour, and so this lesson and passage of information are for everyone who requires a helping hand.

Alternatively, it can be for a single person and soul who imagines I am hiding from them—like a thief—deep within the night.

So, from the moment you open your eyes from sleep, until darkness descends once more at the end of your day, what signs can be seen? What do you need, pray or dream of? Would you like divine inspiration, and if so, in what 'shape or form' should this arrive? What stone needs to be upturned? Is there a guru or religious figurehead which you must visit to progress?

Like a traffic light, are you waiting for it to turn green, as if pausing for my permission to proceed? In addition, why do you wait for anyone or anything in order to step closer to me? Understand that your journey is not a new road or discovery, but is your existing body, and the path you already walk!

For some, the embodiment you find yourself in may be less—or more—than you think you deserve. However, do not despise or over analyse such things, but embrace your current life or situation. Know that in whatever the circumstances, you are never, ever alone. You are 'me' and I am you … remember.

Besides, I cannot take 'light' from anyone of you, as this is the permanent core of your soul. Only you can do this—through some self-fulfilling prophecy—to resemble a lamp covered by a blanket, and live, sleep and exist in the shade … when in fact your light, both internal and external, can shine brighter than a billion Suns.

Please try to rise above any negativity that picks and irritates the body and mind, most of which can be deflected and dissipated by sending out thoughts of love and kindness. Simplicity is invariably the key during times where doubt or anguish raise their ugly head. Simple truths will also provide clarity and enable you to power ahead.

From an early age, children will look for—and need direction—and support. Likewise, spiritual education ought to be undertaken with commitment, passion, and endeavour to help you (the aspirant), in achieving your goal of self-realization and eternal bliss.

So, where does one find such things? Who does one seek counsel with? What books must you read? Do you need to visit sacred sites? Well, realise all these are secondary and only steppingstones towards me. If I am everything, then it is your own free will and conscience which dictates otherwise.

Therefore, by opening your heart, you will identify the love you are and can become. But what can you do if you currently think you're lost or confused? Well, should this be the case, please stop this train of thought and do not let your mind trick you at any stage of your life, because the effort you now make is unquantifiable.

Try to imagine your arrival in a strange and unfamiliar city. Everywhere you look, there are buildings, roads, districts, and suburbs that startle, frighten or even intimidate you. Do you fear crossing the road or boundary into the unknown, or do you forge ahead with the challenge and task of discovery you yourself had set?

Appreciate that by turning within, you will realise and sense my help to make your decisions. Then you'll understand that in reality, those street signs and maps all equate to elements in your life, like your job, house, family, relatives, friends, and so forth. Some of these will go hand in hand; while others will appear to move forward and alone, as if they are separate from you.

Often, these roads will be smooth in your life and deemed pleasurable and happy for you. Then, as a new day dawns, and a corner turned, your entire world may seem to be thrown upside down. Each of you will react differently, of course, and yet it is your own re-action to your 'action'—similar to cause and effect—which will affect and weigh heavily upon your emotional and physical health.

Comprehend too, as you age, those days, weeks, months, and years will fly by ... though the opposite occurs in your childhood and teenage years, where they appeared to pass slowly. Later, as time becomes more significant—during adulthood or retirement—one will distinctly hope to find the truth and destination, and the real meaning for their life.

So, perhaps all you need to do is to travel up the next street, or one could even believe a sign will illuminate above you, bathed in a heavenly glow. Picture some words upon it right now—in your mind's eye—as it might say, 'ONE WAY!' ... 'AHEAD ONLY!' ... 'FOLLOW THE LIGHT!' ... 'THIS IS TRUE!' ... 'JUST BE POSITIVE!'

One may really wonder where this will actually lead you. Could it direct you through the maze of complexity, the jungle of confusion, and the heartache of joy and pain? Indeed, if you decide to pause and reflect upon your own truth, the sign will simply say in bold letters, 'YOURSELF'. This is because the road, path and current lifetime will only guide you towards the reality of you. The journey travelled is the one you created for yourself, both from now, and from the many incarnations of embodiment!

Please understand, you are living this amazing chance and opportunity, which knocks on the door of your soul. So, follow your heart and do what feels right for you within your life, remembering not to hurt anyone or anything, and be a help to whom or whatever your path encounters. While doing so, please try to weather the peaks and troughs of troubled waters with dignity and equanimity, for I will lead you to the safety of the shore, because I love you more than you could ever realise or know.

To conclude for today, know deep within your soul lies the peace and tranquillity beyond your wildest dreams. Once you find me, you will discover yourself, and then you will fully understand and comprehend the clearest and most profound sign of all. Amen."

Robert gave a single chime of the table bell, and thirty minutes of blissful peace followed. I reached for my pen and notepad by my side. Swami materialised before the group, and I bowed my head to acknowledge His presence and Divinity.

He then smiled and said, "Welcome, welcome, welcome. I know and love you all. The circle is protected and guided as always, so be still and let your heart rejoice in my name and energy. Allow peace to wash and rain (reign) over your souls ... so you will sparkle like diamonds and stars." Sai had a brief message for each devotee:

Manny: "My soldier of light, continue to be strong for others around you. My shield called 'faith', will always protect you. Live in love and love life, my friend."

Jan: "Dear daughter, please understand your tears now belong in the past. They will forever cling to the crown of my heart, hanging in suspension until joy is all you can think about."

Kimmy: "Mother Nature beholds you ... as you ground higher energy through Her, to the realms below ... and for those who strive to draw nearer to the light. You are a conduit, so please continue to resonate on different planes."

Kate: "All people like creature comforts, but not always in a material sense. Let your love continue to shine and be the comfort to those who need help, or a shoulder to cry upon. The pillars of truth and fortitude will sustain you."

SYMBOLISM AND COLOUR

Issy: "Have no regrets and live life to the full. Forget time and enjoy the 'living in the moment'. Once ready, your hidden work that you do … and also your joy, will be even greater."

Julie: "Gentle and loving, please continue to reach for the truth … but more importantly, simply allow the truth to reach you. Have no doubt in your mind or life, because destiny will be fulfilled."

Robert: "I made you all in my image. So the negative doesn't exist in peace and love. Your love captured me in your heart, but while a photograph is 'frozen in time' … love will flourish and illuminate, what the 'I' needs to see." (Robert is a brilliant photographer).

Jim: "No one can say they have finished their task. Forget age or appearance, my son. Duty and honour go hand in hand … and you remain in mine."

Swami stood serenely in the centre of the circle. While raising His hand, He spoke once more, "Be at peace … be at peace, I AM I." I looked down at my pen … He was gone. Almost immediately, Robert gave a chime of the bell to conclude the meditation. Some of the group were so deeply entranced, their heads were slumped on their chests. After a minute or so, everyone had realization of their bodies, and gently became aware of their surroundings once more.

Robert gave a prayer of gratitude. Then, whoever felt inclined, would reach for the large white feather (on the small coffee table) in front of us, before sharing their experience from within the peace and silence. Sometimes, a message from their spirit guides—or directly from God's love and light 'hierarchy'—came through for a particular person, too. (I would normally speak last, because the transcribed messages usually took longer to read).

We closed the circle by offering absent healing and personal prayers ... followed by chanting the 'Lokah Samastah' mantra.

> *"Lokah Samastah Sukhino Bhavantu,*
> *Lokah Samastah Sukhino Bhavantu,*
> *Lokah Samastah Sukhino Bhavantu*
>
> *Shanti, Shanti, Shanti!"*

After Vibhuti, Robert and Kate concluded the amazing evening by serving some lovely snacks, along with some very tasty onion bhajis, and samosas. Thank you once again, beloved Swami. Om Sai Ram/Amen.

TRUST AND FAITH

I had noticed that in some of the meditation reports, Swami's spiritual guidance and education (for each of the circle members), appears to be getting longer, which is fabulous! This one is a great example of how His messages, while pertinent to the said recipient ... appear to apply to every seeker of truth!

We all arrived in plenty of time for a quick drink and catch up on each other's news. After a few minutes of silence, we began with Robert's opening prayer, and chanting of the mantra.

"Aum Bhur Bhurvah Suvah
Tat Savitur Varenyam
Bhargo Devasya Dheemahi
Dhiyo yonah Prachodayat."

Followed by the Lesson: **CLARITY**

"I welcome hearts and souls from every form of life to sense and know the truth. Furthermore, I hope—by the end of these few pages—you will find a clearer view of where you are headed and what's needed and required for you to become fulfilled ... and therefore be at peace within yourself.

So, how will you begin or end your day? Will it be with optimism, enthusiasm, and excitement for the challenges which lie ahead?

Or, does a feeling of trepidation, uncertainty, or frustration attempt to grip you? Will this prevent you from experiencing the truth of whom, what, why and where you are at this present time?

If the latter is the case, one could easily visualize a dense fog, rolling down the hills and rising in the valleys. It blurs and attempts to hide your true vision of mind and body, and soul. Sometimes, such days may feel as if there is no escape. They seem to overtake, overwhelm, and confuse you.

However, please try to understand that life can take these turns. These are the days where there appear to be too many decisions to make. I bear witness as you look for the answers to your family, work, or home 'situations'. And many people appear to be wondering around, unable to see the wood from the tress, or even their own hands in front of their face.

You must all realise uncertain times for what they are … temporary and fleeting phases. So, instead of believing that the unknown weakens you, or having negative responses to circumstances with which you assume—often mistakenly—are out of your control, just try to change your mindset.

Only love is permanent. So, whatever is occurring cannot last forever. It does not matter what way you perceive or how you look at it. Hence, like the power of the Sun, which brings light every day to banish darkness, so, too, the mind can refocus to clear these clouds of illusion and confusion. Then, the fog upon those hills and in the valleys below will eventually change to mist. It elevates. To your senses, it will seem to have disappeared—from, and through, and by rays of heat from above, and also from the love within.

Know it is I then, who—through your heart's centre—will empower you to rise above such times, clearing the way with determination and truth to live your life with honesty and integrity. Therefore, please trust and believe your own strength lies inside you. In time, you'll know that what is seen through the eye (I) of the heart can differ greatly from the eyes of your body.

Those true windows—of opportunity—to behave and display the traits of a kind and helpful human being may once have been obscured. Or they seem distant (like blurred far away objects becoming difficult to distinguish), but by removing the impediments of doubt and fear, you will refocus on important decisions and goals, and those many responsibilities in your life.

In fact, every day, your surroundings—and society—will knowingly, or unknowingly, attempt to trick or disguise what is seen, felt, or heard by your senses. If these are not filtered through discretion and morality, or even by one's own faith, such elements enter the mind, becoming displayed once more through desire, anguish, hatred, and fear by what you think and say and do.

It is vital, therefore, to separate the wheat from the chaff. One must pick what feels right for you during work, rest, and play. Sometimes this will be easy, other times not so. For example, imagine for a moment you are listening to relaxing music upon an old cassette tape, which has since become crinkled or twisted … instead of hearing the pure melody or notes, they will only resemble background noise, a distortion in the voice of truth.

So, one needs to iron out, re-tune, and refocus to understand what is being said or portrayed. I can assist and guide you. But I cannot do this for you because your own inner journey—utilising discernment—will need and want to grow through one's own experience to become 'wise'. If I lay all the answers out before you, your own efforts would wish to—and more often than not—take an easier road or route every single time.

Of course, some of you, either for karmic reasons (or to assist other souls), aren't in this position, whereby you constantly have to make difficult choices and decisions on the road ahead. Also, one cannot achieve and attain wisdom through another's eyes or heart. It is the one journey that you must undertake with me, 'together' … for you are not, and never will be, alone.

Therefore, with the aid of these books, but more importantly with my love in your heart—as a guide, teacher, confidant, friend, and companion who is forever within, above, below, and by your side—you can continue with fortitude and determination towards self-realization and bliss … into peace.

Do not idle in your endeavours. Nor become affected by anyone else's influence unless it connects and resonates with your own truth inside. If you feel happiness and contentment—and it brings meaning to you—then all must be well … because negativity, fear, or distrust would make you feel out of sync, apprehensive, and uncertain.

Do not believe this will eternally side-track you; it won't. All truth leads to me. A 'detour' of experience often helps to keep you focused, for it gives prompts and clues about your own inner search and thirst for knowledge. Through discrimination, you can then make the right choices from and through and to the heart.

Comprehend that any limitations are false. They are the subject of the subconscious mind. This only tries to see the future by focusing on the past. It can release negativity through irrational thoughts and subsequently affect your behaviour. That said, it can still protect you. It does this by rationalizing your decisions, stopping you from purposefully harming yourself, unless one is mentally or emotionally impaired through illness, disease, or by various forms of abuse. It is appropriate to always be on your guard. I will help you by being your conscience, which pricks the mind … as well as your intuition, providing those gut feelings swelling over you when something feels right or wrong.

So, if you can trust in me, you will trust in yourself. As we are 'one', you will need no other false declarations of support, to help carry you when days seem tough, and/or when others despair. You can be the strength for those who cannot see the light and wish to cling to you. You can help encourage, motivate, and lead—as and when required to do so—because you know, and also see, the truth both within and out.

With the understanding that 'life' can be what you make of it—even in desperate times—I am there if you look for me. I am the smile, the birdsong, and the lone flower amongst the weeds of discontentment and hurt and anger. I am the softly spoken words to encourage and help, the comforting arm during tears of grief, and the stranger who assists you in the hour of need. Yes, I am the love, the light, and am all things in all places.

I promise I will wipe away and cleanse the anguish of every heart and soul. You will see, feel, and sense me more clearly than ever before. And, because love knows no bounds, it is free from time and distance … all the while permeating, and transcending, every plane and dimension, of energy and vibration.

You are this same power and magnificence. Believe it to be so and nothing, absolutely nothing, can prevent you from making your hopes, dreams, and your eternal goal come true. Finally, today, please appreciate that having clarity of thought is an immense step. It leads to a clearer vision of whom, what, and why you are, and—as mentioned earlier—where you're headed to. Amen."

As soon as the meditation began, the ceiling resembled the firmament above ... full of stars, suns, light, planets, moons ... Creation itself. Swami's face poured forth from a galaxy. "I am here in the name of truth and love. Indeed, for you, to you, through you and from you ... we are 'one'. Time is irrelevant. Each second, minute, hour, day, week, month and year are by-products of the mind. The heart and soul is all that matters, and I send this message to you all."

Kimmy: "Witness the stars, galaxy, space ... and the universe. Everything is but atoms of my fingernail. Do not worry whether your actions bear fruit, it's your thoughts and love that rides the energy waves of Creation. Dear child, everything dissipates but this. Let everything else fade, and simply go with the flow across my ocean of love. We go hand in hand, remember?"

Kate: "Your body is a vessel ... a ship upon the sea of emotion. I am the power in the sails. My breath guides you and carries you to the shore of your destiny and goal ... your timeless home inside my heart. Do not worry. Do not fear. You'll never go overboard. I am your safety net, and the eternal buoy to cling to in any cause or need."

Julie: "The sand of time drift endlessly by, but you do not need to measure whether one's life is full, half-full or empty. With love, you are always fulfilled, and even though life can cause doubt to rise ... know my child that I do not and will not neglect you. All trials and tribulations carry you forward to where you need to be and for what you require to experience. Therefore, what is there to be concerned about when you know, deep within, that everything you sense and feel is perfection? I will 'lighten' your cares and burdens. Trust in me to help you and carry you upon your journey."

Robert: "Power and energy and truth and light are all part of my essence which is no more than a reflection of your own. The Earth, planets, solar systems and beyond are all sustained through my heart. Hence, I sustain you …but you sustain me, too. Your life may sometimes seem to drift by, but each and every day brings it's reason and purpose no matter how small or insignificant it may appear to be.

The sun and it's warmth, the land and mountains and trees, the seas which span the Earth, and the deserts, which appear dry and unforgiving places, are all no more than the microcosm and macrocosm, of me. No one needs to concern themselves whether they are big or small in the grand scheme of things, because every grain of sand is important … for it makes one whole. Let your love drift where it will, for it shall fall and nurture life exactly when required to do so. May your life continue to be a snapshot of truth for others to witness and be guided to me."

As if on cue, with the meditation due to end … Baba raised His hand (as if to say farewell) and said, "Allow love and light to shine through you all. Be at peace, always and forever."

We said our prayers and sent absent healing, then gave thanks to Sai. Circle:

> *"Lokah Samastah Sukhino Bhavantu,*
> *Lokah Samastah Sukhino Bhavantu,*
> *Lokah Samastah Sukhino Bhavantu*
>
> *Shanti, Shanti, Shanti!"*

Robert shared Vibhuti with us, before he and Kate served their light refreshments and snacks. Some devotees discussed their experiences while holding the feather of truth, then I proceeded to read Swami's messages. What an amazing meeting! Om Sai Ram/Amen.

In this next meditation, Swami actually mentions the title of this book! And, as I collate all of these notes, I am reminded that this is the first time I have read them, since they were written! I'm so sorry Swami. Then, as I'm typing ... a notion flashes through my mind, 'Divine' timing. And, as everything has its place and purpose ... I believe this is it.

The group are already to start. We are calm and peaceful after our greetings and opening prayers and mantra:

> *"Aum Bhur Bhurvah Suvah*
> *Tat Savitur Varenyam*
> *Bhargo Devasya Dheemahi*
> *Dhiyo yonah Prachodayat."*

Lesson: **TRUST AND FAITH**

"Welcome again to 'stillness' and some contemplation time, enabling you to reflect and clear out those thoughts, which inhibit clarity and will soon bring you peace. The working day is done, so be still and rejoice in the calmness of your true self, for you and I are 'one'.

Understand my love washes over you all, but many do not sense, or become 'still', in order to appreciate and grow within it. Everyone will do so, but not until they realise who, what, and why they are a spark of divinity.

Tonight, you can now place your earthly existence on pause, to let light and truth rain in. This will cleanse any doubts, fears and misapprehensions occurring during your day, so do not concern yourself with minor ills or worries, for these are trivial when all is said and done.

Remember, these only take place because you are being 'tested' by 'spirit', to establish one's inherent code of conduct, and whether the individual or the masses can prevail and 'rise above it'. Indeed, as I bear witness to the reaction of such things, this makes perfect sense.

Therefore, it is best to avoid negativity, and those who are unable to express or share the love in their heart, too. You can achieve this diplomatically, without a blank refusal or a curse from the tongue. And, if you live by the truth inside you, recognising ill-fated paths and actions becomes second nature.

Remember, being positive also attracts the same, where spiritual education and guidance is concerned. However, the expression 'opposites attract' is only true of the physical and impermanent world in which your embodiment lives at this time.

So now I ask you, do you trust in how you act and think? Do you follow your intuition and those 'gut' feelings? If you do, you are acknowledging the unbreakable bond connecting all creation. Please realise, when you place this trust in me, there is no fear. Living without fear brings you peace. Within peace, you find bliss, and in this state of being, your true 'self' shines like a supernova, with magical stardust spiralling and spinning in all directions. In reality, these words cannot express or do justice to such beauty.

In addition, many opportunities throughout your life will come and go, so grasp those that ring true, and which resonate inside you. When you engage tasks with, by, and through truth, then nothing is impossible to achieve. Only the limits you set or propose to yourselves, can prevent the goal of attaining ascension.

Therefore, by trusting in all you truly are, you can reach far beyond what you can or cannot see. Dismiss those false limitations and boundaries, erected only by the insecurities of an illusionary mind. Push these aside with your love, to trust me to give and help you with what you need and require, not in what you think you want and desire.

Remember, you do not need to travel far from your home or disappear deep into a forest to discover me. Finding me is easy, because I am already within and outside of you … as I am all things. In fact, I am the stars at night, shining light through the darkness. I am every leaf and rock. I am earth, fire, water, and air. I am the wind brushing against your face. I am the peace and tranquillity you crave. All these I am, and you are too … no separation or division, only oneness in all.

However, people's thoughts of doubt and despair can still linger both on the 'earth-plane', and upon many vibration levels of energy. "How can I believe? What proof can you provide for me? Why do you let so many lives suffer in pain or anguish?" Please appreciate, I am not blind to any heart that aches or breaks, for I bear witness, sense, and live through them all.

You can wash away your ills and concerns in an instant, but you would not learn, or grow. Upon a soul level, mortal man cannot achieve, or ease, their karmic imbalance this way. So, faith is the power to guide, and carry you, throughout 'life', and its seemingly impossible burdens of work, family, and your general well-being within society. However, many religions from scores of nations use this gift without discernment, and then faith resembles a byword, or phrase, to indoctrinate hearts and minds.

I am not stating people should throw away any aspect of a religion or cultural inheritance they have grown to know, and one should not consider, or decree, a life more sacred than someone or something else's is. Considering this, who and what should you believe in? Does your current thought process, and belief system, enable you to be who you are, deep within?

Now, I do not wish to antagonise or offend any being or life, but only the truth (and its reflection) can make another place or person feel this way. Rather this; believe me and so believe in yourself, because true faith in love and light is so magnificent, powerful, beautiful, and amazing, and has no bounds. 'Faith can move mountains' is a saying known too many, but how deep lays this truth, buried inside your hearts over the centuries and eons of time?

My message from this day forth is for you to dig deep into your spiritual core, to grasp and behold this golden nugget. Keep its truth and power close to you each minute of every day. It will never let you down, for as you search and pray, and through your actions, words, and deeds of love, I will polish and smooth the rough edges of your soul's experiences.

So, please have faith in me. Never doubt me, for I do not place doubt in you. My strength will be your strength. My love is your love, and my light is your light. You will shine eternally within me, and your divinity shall remain forever. Show all whom you meet the truth inside you and become a guiding hand to those who doubt or fear, living without faith, even in themselves.

For those who are still unsure, I request a leap of faith does not require you to risk your health (or those of your loved ones), or anything at all to do with your well-being. It is a gap and space, which only appears to exist between you and me. This is unreal, because my love for you is an eternal bridge, which cannot ever crumble. Therefore, seek me by taking just one small step upon it; for I promise you, I will carry you forever into everlasting bliss. Amen."

Robert softly rang the table bell for the mediation period to begin. I soon started to write as Baba appeared in front of the fireplace. "Bless you all ... I am here as always. Be still, be still, be still. The passage of time brings friends and family together, both on the physical plane and upon the 'lighter' levels and planes.

Love is strong there and here, and with the group you may call a circle ... a circle of trust and hope and friendship. My love is as fragrant and as powerful as one may deem it to be. Hence, rest and become aware of me ... within your heart and mind and senses.

Let the aroma and nectar of my heart, cleanse the negativity and worries of the day. Bask in my light, which reveals the wisdom each of you need, or desire. I am here ... I am here ... I am here, always."

Keith: "For richer or poorer and in sickness and in health. This is the vow of our own universal marriage of your soul and my heart. Do not fret or stress or worry. Keep strong in your mind and heart. I am with you every step you take, remember?"

Kimmy: "Dear child, let wisdom flow through your heart and soul, and allow this to influence the mind. Opportunities to express our love may come and go, but the more gentle, subtle times will become even more apparent to you, in the days and weeks and months ahead. Do not concern yourself of the how, why, what and when, one of my prompts will be your guide. Trust in me."

Kate: "Like a pearl in a shell (deep within the ocean), most cannot see the beauty inside. Do not worry about being on 'display' ... love needs no medals or banners to show the true love inside you. A smile or a gentle touch of the hand expresses the truth of who and what you are ... Divinity, remember?"

Julie: "Blessings and peace be upon you. Places to be and no time for this or that and the other. Life is hectic and can seem too fast paced to allow you to be the 'real' you, or so you think! Some days you have to juggle family, life, work and home responsibilities and it can appear to become all too much. Well, I am the spare pair of hands to assist your workload and tasks to complete. You only need to think of me. Call me ... ask me to help you and I will be there for you, I promise."

Manny: "Pastures new beckon, but the work of the heart shall continue. Let it radiate and shine and touch a new nation and new hearts and souls. Build your new home upon strong foundations of faith and trust and hope and love. Remember, as always, your true home of your heart provides eternal rest for your soul."

Jan: "Blessings and good wishes to you as you continue your earth's journey in more ways than one! Time and distance are irrelevant to me, and no matter wherever you lay your head ... I am watching over you. Allow your mind some breathing space ... declutter what is not relevant in your life and your home. You will always have what you need to be able to share the 'real estate' of your heart and soul. Keep strong even in testing times and let me be your strength you can rely upon."

Robert: "Walk the good walk, talk the good talk. Let your feelings become free ... more free than you can ever thought possible. Allow your love to fly beyond the walls of your home, through the physical plane, dream state and into the higher realms, too. What you share in truth returns ten-fold. Remember to always speak what you feel. I am with you to protect and guide and nurture your soul ... forever."

Swami raised His right hand, and just as the meditation ended, said, "Be at peace all of you. We are one." Then, He disappeared.

Prayers, absent healing and salutations concluded the wonderful meeting. Once Vibhuti was shared, each devotee spoke with the feather of truth in their hand. Circle:

> *"Lokah Samastah Sukhino Bhavantu,*
> *Lokah Samastah Sukhino Bhavantu,*
> *Lokah Samastah Sukhino Bhavantu*
>
> *Shanti, Shanti, Shanti!"*

It was such a blessing to provide Sai's guidance for everyone, before having a lovely cup of tea and snacks. Thank you beloved Swami for your grace and kindness and love, we are forever grateful ... Om Sai Ram/Amen.

After a long day at work, a quick bath and a bite to eat, I set off for Peterborough. Half-way there I was stuck in a traffic jam, and vehicles tailed back for over a mile. There wasn't even an accident, so goodness knows what the hold-up was. I was so looking forward to the Circle, and by Swami's grace and blessings and guidance, I arrived just in the nick of time! Robert made me a quick cup of tea, and we started straight away, with prayers and the Gayathri Mantra:

> *"Aum Bhur Bhurvah Suvah*
> *Tat Savitur Varenyam*
> *Bhargo Devasya Dheemahi*
> *Dhiyo yonah Prachodayat."*

Lesson: **PATHWAYS**

"I welcome all those who have seemingly 'travelled' from near or far—overcoming trepidation and fear—to become a witness to my love. So, do you feel that you have overcome some great distance? Or, have you (in truth), drawn closer to me in no time at all … as in the blink of an eye ('I')?

Please comprehend that there are so many roads and pathways in all of Creation. Therefore, it is often called the 'pathless' path. Each provides a 'choice less' choice, or moreover, a chance to become whom I really meant you to be. Understand though, that throughout your current embodiment, it is so natural to look and take the so-called easier route. It is an attempt to evade all of life's pitfalls, in the belief it can somehow bring you more quickly—or closer—to me.

Others, meanwhile, accept the way forward with challenges being met head on. So, when you embark upon the voyage of discovery called life—with both integrity and honesty—then truth not only becomes your guide but also your protection. Like an umbrella, it will cast aside the fall of emotions which flow incessantly from the mind, trying to influence and direct your heart.

In contrast, your sojourn—you could read this as 'soul-journey'—really has only one route or path to undertake. It is the inner path and is your very own. Hence, no written word, guru, or saint, can walk it for you. Neither would you wish them to. As a result, if you see—or ever feel—that there's a secret or divine explanation, or indeed any other magical formulae which explains that you can have access to reality by any other means other than through thy heart, then they are surely mistaken.

That said, only you yourself can make that judgment call. Simply accept what resonates within you and what doesn't. Remember, I will never be your judge and jury. You are each forever your own.

So, where do you believe you are right now? Do you sense or feel mystified by circumstances around you at this present time? Are you uncertain of your thoughts and actions? Have you stopped trusting in yourself and in me? Indeed, it can be natural for many of you across the 'earth-plane' to feel uncertain right now, in times of economic and global turmoil, though perhaps it would be unnatural to feel anything else. Or would it?

As this is an important period upon the Earth's calendar, millions of people (over Easter) will wish to refocus—perhaps even re-align—their thoughts and hearts ... remembering Lord Jesus upon the cross and his resurrection.

But no matter what religion you follow, one's faith can be strengthened, or even renewed at any time, but especially more so now. How much emphasis it bears in your life is also down to the individual and your own feelings and emotions flowing through your being. This will help you feel more—or possibly less—connected to me and to love, which is the source and energy of all things.

Appreciate that love is uncomplicated, being simple in its manifestation of, from, and throughout all creation. This is the one path that—if followed—will never lead you astray, or into disarray. It is the beacon of truth ... an eternal flame, just like the spark of divinity within your own heart's centre.

It does not need any man-made or impermanent method to light the way ahead. No 'streetlamps' are required to see where you are going. Your own pathway is already illuminated if you can trust all is as it should be.

Do you ever feel or think that I do not know what you need or want? Are you currently assuming that decisions you make are entirely your own? Can you hear me as your conscience, or those gut feelings or intuition? And are you actually relying upon your mind alone to discover what it thinks are the safest and most desirable routes to take you forward, based on your own experiences or those of others around you?

Mm ... people will often state that if you do not have a plan, then you are planning to fail. But in whose eyes, and by what standard or expectation, is this? One must realise that it is your own responsibility to understand all paths lead to me, so how can you fail? You only need to decide—and finally comprehend—that not only are you more than a 'body,' but you are precious beyond compare.

Understand too, all the accolades and so-called success given by one person upon another, or even by society, are all by-products of life. They come to fruition, though all will become residues of the past. Unlike love, which is forever glorified and polished by my grace.

Therefore, by striving and in living to be the best human being you can be, with truth, non-violence, right conduct, peace—and with love—all the exterior trappings of earthly success, whether this is fame or fortune, one's health or friendships, can all individually (or collectively) cross the road that you take.

In contrast, when one walks or travels along negative routes, beholding traits of hate, jealousy, anger, pride, and ego, then one's life, whether past, present, or future—if so required—will reflect this. Every soul and their karmic burden must be dissolved and eradicated, placed into the fire of truth, so that the living flame can turn the imbalance into ash.

It is self-perpetuating. Goodwill brings goodwill—and God's will—and although ill-favoured deeds may seem to be hidden or forgotten, I remember them all, upon your own scales of justice and truth. Everything is balanced. Effect always follows cause, no matter whom, what, where, or why in all of existence. Consequently, do not deem yourself too small or too big, somehow thinking that one is above or below such things, as the eyes of truth are forever watching over you.

Do not think that you can keep a secret from your true 'self' either … or from me. Likewise, do not feel that one deserves more—or less—than you think you (or they) ever should. When you fully understand and know that I love you beyond comprehension, self-realization becomes the reality. This will lead you to every aspect of your life.

So, by comprehending that you are I and I am you, the weight, and burdens that you have brought with you—and may have collected—upon your current pathway, will fall away (or so you may think), for it is I who will carry them instead, with my blessing and 'All That I Am'. I do not separate you from me. I will only ever let you carry what you can bear at any one time … and this is my promise.

Some days you will feel you are trying to drag a dead weight behind you, with the struggle immense, and the pressure of responsibility or desire almost unbearable. As there are so many types of pain, be it physical, mental, or emotional, some will feel worse than others. But you only need to think of me and feel me in your heart to know that I am right there with, besides, above, below, within, and out of you. Therefore, how can you ever be alone?

You are my friend, brother, sister, husband, wife, partner, King or Queen … and everything beyond and in between. You can, from this day forth, resurrect your flame of faith, hope, and charity. For together—as one—we can not only illuminate your own pathway ahead but enable any aspect of life that may have fallen by the wayside, to sense and see the aspect of true life and love. This eternally shines from your heart through my own. In doing so, you thereby assist and guide them towards finding their own pathway too. Amen."

The meditation began with the chime of the bell, and Swami appeared almost immediately! "Peace and blessings to you all. Your presence is a present ... a gift pre-sent through your hearts of love and light. These form a Circle of truth, and one of hope and joy and friendship, for all those who join or gather to listen and grow. Remember, each and every soul always learns something ... no matter how insignificant words or thoughts are deemed to be. Tonight, new energy–full of colour and resonance–will elevate the mind, heal the heart by dissolving anxiety, stress, or fear. Be still and allow your souls time to rest."

Julie: An orange glow emanated from Baba. "I envelope you with my robe (gown). Know you are protected upon the path you tread, for you are never alone. Though the sun rises or sets upon the horizon, allow your hopes and dreams to fly beyond these notions of any boundaries. We are one, and I am always with you."

Keith: Sai face seemed to be overshadowed/joined by Jesus's! Keith appeared to be dressed in in burgundy, a red wine colour. "You receive Christ's energy ... the blood of Christ. Like the last supper ... partake in me. I am the Son ... I am the way, the truth and the life. Remember me, I am always with you. So, do not fear and keep strong in all you do."

Kimmy: A swirl of blue powder descends from Baba's hand. "I am the ocean and you are the wave ... no separation. Blue will refresh and cool the emotional fires of frustration and anger which can test you when least expect it. The energy now sent to you can assist you by easing the concerns of the mind. Like a gentle stream, allow it to cleanse and wash away the worries of your day."

Kate: "I provide green for calm and reassurance both physically and mentally. It will take you to a meadow, woodland or forest. The healing energy of creation will sooth your body and mind and bring freshness to your whole being. You could say it will be like a breath of fresh air, so become strengthened with the vitality of life. Becoming youthful in thought shall bring much joy."

Robert: "You'll sense yellow and brightness, like the sun with warmth from its rays. Imagine yourself as the same ... reflecting and radiating light and love far and wide. Your soul's presence is felt beyond the boundaries of what you imagine you can experience through the senses. Mo matter day or night, allow your being to radiate the truth of your divinity."

Swami began to slowly pace back and forth inside the circle, and concluded his message. "A rainbow surrounds you all, it unifies every soul who is here today. We are whole." The chime of the table bell immediately followed for the meditation to close.

What a peaceful and enlightening evening indeed. To also bear witness to Jesus's presence and energy was incredible to say the least. We are all truly humbled. Absent healing was sent out along with our prayers and salutations. Circle:

"Lokah Samastah Sukhino Bhavantu,
Lokah Samastah Sukhino Bhavantu,
Lokah Samastah Sukhino Bhavantu

Shanti, Shanti, Shanti!

With Vibhuti partaken, each devotee held the white feather and discussed their meditation, then I spoke about Swami and Jesus's wonderful presence ... bringing precious gifts of colour and energy to all. Thank you, thank you, thank you. Om Sai Ram/Amen."

TRUST AND FAITH

Due to Roberts health (and also very bad weather), a couple of meetings had to be postponed. So, after what seemed an age, the Circle finally met again. You know that feeling you get, when true friends and family (who haven't seen each other for a long time), it's like you've never been apart. Well, this is how this Sai Baba group made you feel.

We had a good catch up between us. I also mentioned an enlightening/spiritual dream that I had received, since our last meeting. Then, after getting comfortable and preparing ourselves for the meditation and spiritual work to come. Robert said opening prayers. And we chanted the important mantra:

> *"Aum Bhur Bhurvah Suvah*
> *Tat Savitur Varenyam*
> *Bhargo Devasya Dheemahi*
> *Dhiyo yonah Prachodayat."*

Lesson: **TEST**

"From before the moment of your birth into physical embodiment, you will have trials and tribulations to deal with and overcome. These are only situations or events to help you grow as a human being and soul. How you deal with—and more importantly—how you accept them; will show your spiritual development and growth as a soul and spark of Divinity.

However, please note that you have the same equal chance—and the choice—to test what you receive from any source of help, whether it is through the physical, mental, or emotional aspects of your being. Therefore, if the spiritual guidance and education can be heard or read—or in any way touches your senses—you may establish whether it is just, and good, and if it comes to, through, or by you in the name of love and light.

For a moment, try to cast your mind back to biblical times and the Lord's 40 days between his resurrection and ascension. Did Thomas not have his 'doubt' removed by placing his hand and fingers into and upon Christ's wounds? Jesus wanted—and also needed him—to have his proof, so it would become part of his story (history), which unfolded to leave all souls upon the 'earth-plane' with the same task to believe, and therefore 'live'.

Now, in this modern age, what will make each of you continue to believe and grow? What evidence will a person require to understand their life and true purpose? For some, nothing is necessary. For others, perhaps even love—which can glisten and shine like a beacon within a darkened room—is still not enough. The truth can't be seen as the heart, and 'I', pretend to be divided.

Please comprehend that it is good to question (and also test) every source where guidance is requested. Remember, too, within all dimensions of time and space, no element of light can ever be offended. So, do not be afraid or at all worried by continually asking for confirmation if that is what you need.

As so many of you are working upon different levels—which does not make someone better than another in any way, shape, or form—a soul may recognize me and my love within any form of life. Others, meanwhile, may feel the truth via dreams, visions, or by gazing upon natural (or even unnatural) phenomena which materialize within the impermanent world where you live.

TRUST AND FAITH

Perhaps it is being a witness to a solar eclipse, the northern lights, shooting stars, or even a comet which can help one question or believe they are part of something far greater than themselves. Therein lays the clue which I often reiterate. It is through your own self-realization you will obtain bliss and peace. I can simplify this even further still, which is to simply 'know thyself'.

You will know what 'truth' is at all times, because it will resonate inside you. When the answer you seek—and the illumination and guidance you need, seem to click and just fall into place—within mind, heart, and soul … it will feel natural. You do not need to force yourself. Nor fight against how you feel to make something both understandable and meaningful.

So, let life come to you. Try to approach each day with zest and zeal, not with dread, anguish, or uncertainty. This way, you can see time as less of a test, and more of an opportunity, to become a shining example … of who you really are.

Armed with this knowledge, you can move forward with a conviction that all is well and as it should be. No need to fret, with thoughts you should do something else, or that you have not achieved what your mind insists you could have done.

Indeed, the world around you constantly judges or looks to criticize the results of someone's deeds or actions. People forget to see the effort in the part one may have played. Is it really about getting success and winning all the time, whereby second place, or being part of the so-called 'also-rans', becomes a crime?

Know that each of you has abilities. Some are unique in different fields and in diverse ways. As per character and make-up, the body may have many types of personality, but within you are all divine. Not everyone has to strive to be the best in the world, as you are all 'stars' to me.

Practice does not always make perfect. To enforce or place pressure of any kind can prove very harmful, especially to the young. This, of course, is not the same as encouragement, discipline, and endeavour, which are all traits one can either accept or not.

A mother or father who wishes to see their offspring rise to the top of a profession or skill is fine, but the test is not theirs. Hence, the child's desire for success may not always be the same as their own. What is important is that life's tests are for each and for all.

I have stated frequently that I am not your judge or jury, for you are each your own. As such, do I therefore wish for you to witness the truth? Of course, I do. Would I rather you understand and have faith in the real and true 'you', reaching ascension in this lifetime, instead of continual rebirth and death … absolutely.

Therefore, please realise, that you are the very gift of love, which wishes to express itself. Through angels, saints, and my presence among you all, I have already shown you the way. Jesus stated you are all made in my image—your divinity—so how many years (or lifetimes) does it take for the penny to drop? This is not criticism, as it would be like chastising and criticizing my 'self' as I am I! No, these are only words on a page. It is always down to you to decide what to do with the time you have been given.

Understand, by taking a backward step, you will actually take more than one step forward, but how, and what do I mean? Well, as discussed, many times before, when you trust yourself, you must therefore also trust me. That being the case, appreciate that I am working through you.

You are not constantly the 'do-er'. This doesn't get you off the proverbial hook, but means that if you can allow your hands to be mine, your thoughts to be my thoughts, and so on and so forth, only 'good' will ensue.

TRUST AND FAITH

If you can believe I am in you, and am also within your friend, neighbour, and family members, wouldn't you always try to be and do your best? Hence, by serving through your work, rest, and play within society, you are also serving me. And, if you should feel something has gone wrong, the result turning out to someone's disapproval, I will then accept all consequences as my burden, not yours.

Please know, you truly have to believe and make the effort in what you do, though. Half-hearted gestures of goodwill, or to make the result for one's own gain, only continues—or worsens—Karmic imbalance. Therefore—and ultimately within this process—the world can indeed become a much brighter, cleaner, safer place when all souls lose their selfishness, replacing it with selflessness.

And so, what events or tasks have you completed today? Did they test your mind, body, or even perhaps your heart? Could you have said, acted, or thought in a more positive way? Was there an opportunity to help someone or something less fortunate than you? Appreciate that life can be as beautiful and as glorious as you wish to make it. It makes no difference where, or in what skin, you are born. If you can live with, and through, good conduct and peace and love and truth, then your own life can glow, and become, amazingly colourful.

Everyone has a choice, though some do 'experience' more often than others. Likewise, there will always be those who 'have', and there will always be the 'have-nots', but the Sun warms and shines upon every face just the same. Likewise, a smile and laughter also transcend any language or continent, plane, or dimension.

The ultimate test cannot be swapped or exchanged, bargained for, or given away. It is each your very own. All have love inside them.

This is a fact. As I have explained before, even a madman loves someone or something. Believe I am within and with you always—so take and pass the test—and in simply knowing yourself ... and you will find you're already there. Amen."

After the reading, immense calm and peace descended upon us. It was palpable. The thirty minutes of silence started, and Swami blessed us with His presence straight away! "Welcome. Be still. Be true. Be you. Know I am here and there and everywhere. Do not fear when I am near. I am here to guide you. Remember, the threads of my robe surround and protect you. My love dances inside your heart's. All is well, be at peace, always."

Kimmy: "Take my hand, and place your faith and trust and heart, in mine. The path you tread, may seem to direct you away from familiar surroundings, but this is only because your love is often needed in new places. Remember to heed your intuition, as these are the seeds of truth I have placed inside your consciousness."

Kate: "Hello dear child, forget what you think you cannot do and now focus on what you want ... your desire, your creativity. My love and light is your new palette, so remember to express your feelings through what you draw and paint. The colours of the rainbow will shine through your emotions ... but only if you accept and embrace them. Be vibrant and bright and your love will shine through always."

Julie: "For most, family responsibilities can be draining or even a chore. The wise, know differently, because the love and care which pours from the well of your heart remain without limits. Remember you are strong, and the light pours from the cup of truth and flows through you ... to quench the need in those who require physical, mental, or emotional support. There is no burden you have to face alone. I am but a heartbeat away. Speak to me. Ask me for whatever assistance you may need. I am always near you, i am within, without, above, below, in front and behind. I will forever be the strength you need, just believe."

Robert: "The eye of truth needs no lens to focus or view different viewpoints, or determine right from wrong. The mind, for all its desires to guide you from events of the past, can't tell you or advise you of the future. The only focus you will ever need is through the heart. And, when you listen to it, you see more clearly than you ever thought possible. Your soul has no barriers to overcome and hence, when you embrace the wisdom inside you, you will gain greater foresight into where your path shall take you. In addition, remember I'm with you every step you take, whether it's familiar or unfamiliar ground. The protection (if required) is always there for you too, so become more open minded (and open hearted) to things that seem knew."

The chime of the bell to end the meditation coincided with Swami raising his hand ... as if to say 'goodbye' for now. I immediately reached for the feather and asked the group if I could share the individual guidance with them straight away. It just seemed important to do so for some reason. Each person also described their meditations, before Robert gave us all some Vibhuti. Circle:

"Lokah Samastah Sukhino Bhavantu,
Lokah Samastah Sukhino Bhavantu,
Lokah Samastah Sukhino Bhavantu

Shanti, Shanti, Shanti!"

Prayers and healing and our eternal thanks to Sai proceeded tea and coffee and nibbles. The drive home from Peterborough was full of thoughts and blessings for our continued Circle … made possible only by, and through, Swami's grace. Om Sai Ram/Amen.

This early spring Circle from 2019 provided brilliant guidance for members of the group. I hope you will enjoy the messages that were transcribed, and can relate to them in your own life in some way, shape or form. Greetings and prayers were said before with the mantra:

"Aum Bhur Bhurvah Suvah
Tat Savitur Varenyam
Bhargo Devasya Dheemahi
Dhiyo yonah Prachodayat."

Lesson: **RESURRECTION**

"This is an apt title for a Friday, indeed this 'Good Friday'. So, let go of your mind, and do not let it impart new thoughts, concerns, or any form of anxiety over you at this time. In fact, draw down, deep within yourself, and acknowledge the connection, which can never be erased between you and me … for I am I, we are all one, forever and a day.

Please understand, there are people, souls and beings who set aside a space in their hearts, not only to contemplate upon such things today but also debate the Easter 'period' itself. For many, each day will roll into the next, the hands of a clock constantly turning, while others find their faith, trust and hope renewed, reborn, and you could even say—resurrected.

Comprehend this does not mean I favour one religion or deem any land or country to be greater—or more purposeful—than another. Those thoughts are within 'man's' consciousness and brain but bear no relevance to a heart of love and truth. No matter what colour, creed, nationality, or even whether you are male or female in bodily garment, all may use these words of guidance and sustenance freely and equally.

Appreciate too, as you go about your daily tasks, time is becoming more precious, because each family home across the globe can house new whirlwinds of pressure, stress, and confusion. This leads to friction, unhappiness, and uncertainty between all members of society, so please use this moment to pause and reflect, and to re-evaluate your reasons for being and living.

In fact, the desires of the impermanent world need to be reined in, and not expanded beyond one's control. I do not state you cannot be comfortable in your life, for all should be, but reiterate, there is enough of 'everything' for every man, woman, and child upon the Earth.

Remember, each person and soul should realise that by continually striving to earn money—to buy more 'things'—will only mean more work. It is self-perpetuating and can be destructive as the exterior tries to subdue the interior of you. Shadows of doubt and confusion can then attempt to block out the light, which leads you God-ward (inward) ... where all your true needs are met.

Okay then, so having mentioned 'resurrection', comprehend this day will always be remembered when Jesus 'died'. (Remember, to believe in this is your own decision). Indeed, while he cried out, "Why hast thou forsaken me?" ... I suffered too, as do all mothers and fathers who feel pain when their own child is hurting. Please appreciate, you are never alone, separate, or ever divided from me. I am with you constantly, through your sadness and failings, and within your joy and triumphs.

Comprehend I am but a thought away. So, my help, my love and my embrace are there for you. I shall arrive in a smile, in your laughter, or by a helping hand to lift you up. I am with you in the sunrise as the light shines upon your face, or within the breeze and wind which cools your skin. I will be the water that quenches your thirst too, therefore, I am with you always, in all ways. All you have to do is to trust, and ask me.

For some, I remain a mystery, an enigma, or even a fictitious God. Indeed, in countless different languages and spoken tongue, there are hearts who cannot currently 'see,' for false fear and illusion temporarily blinded them. One day, though, all will see clearly with the eyes of the body, mind, and soul in unison—just as they should be. They will know me in all walks of life and by every heart because truth will prevail, sending 'light' to pierce the darkness and rise through doubt and despair.

Know that Jesus rose from the tomb of death to reveal peace, bliss, and self-realization. This is your goal, to remove the cloak and veil of death and fear, and release yourself from the treadmill of rebirth. You can achieve this, but you must make your choice, now that you realise your will is free.

Understand too, humanity is the conduit … who utilizes the energy and vibrations between the Earth and sky. These are not separate, as they are always in contact with each other. In addition, because all things distribute and share positive and negative energy, how each individual person lives—and uses what is both 'within' and 'out'—has a marked effect upon them and their surroundings, too.

This power spontaneously rises from the Earth through the force of water, air, fire, or even the land, which cracks, bursts, or erupts. Fear, anxiety, anger, and frustration in human thoughts cause these in catastrophic ways. But I am still there, throughout moments of panic, terror, desperation, sadness, and loneliness, as well as those so-called good times in your life.

Therefore, I request, from the flames of fire burning brightly inside you, to know the truth. Like a candle shining within a darkened room, I am seen in all directions, so you do not need to ask where I am, as I am all of you. In another simple analogy, consider me as both a spoonful of sugar and a glass of water. If they were mixed, you could not see the sugar, so does this mean it does not exist? I am the ocean and the wave, which merges constantly, remember.

Right now, put down the burden of all of your cares. I promise you, I will pick up the crosses to bear myself, so put your trust in me—and in yourself—to move forward into the light, with the shadows of doubt falling further behind you each day.

Symbolically, may the crown of thorns prick your mental consciousness, bursting the balloon of any inflated ego to tarnish the soul's brightness. Let the blood from Christ's limbs flow through your own veins, and bring the light of the 'Son' into your hearts. And, his body, which bore the sins of—and for—the world, became a reminder, that I will always forgive, and love you. It is for you all ... who need to love, and forgive, each other.

So too, may the robe wrapped around the Lord be known as the blanket of truth and protection. ... and I have placed this around you all, yes, for every one of you. Therefore, even in your darkest hour, feel its warmth, comfort, strength, and compassion in the knowledge it will constantly flow and envelop you, because it is only a thought away. I am I, and so I am you and you are me ... the Father, the Son, and the Holy Ghost.

There is so much more for you all to learn, as we have barely scratched the surface, but just like the phoenix rising from the ashes, this very minute, hour, and day can be the new you, a new beginning of your life. Understand the power of the physical body can never compare with the essence and energy of the immeasurable truth within you. Through the resurrection of your own reality, you can nourish and cherish and believe it, and it will truly fulfil your life. Amen"

We all sat comfortably, as the meditation period was about to begin. After a minute or two, Robert rang the table bell which resonated through the silence. Swami soon came forth bringing immense calm and peace into the room. I knew we were all protected from any negativity especially at this time.

"Welcome. A circle of truth is without limits, boundless. Inside it, you are protected and guided too. As you sink further into your heart, become more aware of our connection to each other and to God's love. At this Easter time, may your souls be raised further towards the light, an increase of energy and vibration to help bring a new dawn to those who live in darkness and fear. We are one always."

Keith: "The Spice of Life. May each day provide you with the necessary ingredients to accomplish what you need, and when. Like a meal, you prepare what is required and therefore one must ready yourself for what you wish to achieve … by utilising not only your mind, but also your heart. Life can seem sweet or sour to most people, but illusions of what is thought of as good or bad need to be dissolved into the ocean of one's emotions. Just as in cooking, timing is everything. So, you will always receive guidance exactly when it's required."

Kimmy: "The Path of Choice. Left, right, front or back … decisions, decisions, decisions. No matter what occurs in your life, one must always take the right path. But, how do you know if you embark in the right direction? You only need to trust that I am with you always, and therefore, whether the path you take at any given time is smooth or rocky, do not fear, for I am closer than near. Be certain that whatever route you take, the decision is based on love and in faith."

Kate: "Turn within. If I asked you to draw, would you automatically pick up a pencil? Possibly, but this is not a test, rather an invitation ... for you to continue to draw 'within' oneself. Here, your inner child wishes to express itself like a picture on canvas. Once you embrace and nurture the spirit within, the creative element of your being will shine and bloom so brightly. You will become unrecognisable, perhaps to those you know ... but to me, you will be blossoming into the true child and spark and soul you were born to be. Remember, to let your creative heart flow, always."

Julie: "Forget Space and time, as distance and the journeys you travel each day within the material world is but the microcosm of your own world you have created around you. Your heart can fly to whatever it needs to be. I place no red light or speed restrictions to inhibit the desires of your soul. I strengthen your resolve, so that you continue to evolve. Even though you carry passengers to where they believe they want to be, each person's soul is on their own journey of self-realisation. Your already ahead, you just need to keep going!"

NB (Julie is currently a bus/coach driver!)

Robert: "Wishes and Dreams. No boundaries are placed before or after your heart and soul. Whether day or night, your soul can float, beyond the ether. I am the ship to sail you across the oceans of time and space and dimensions. You embarked on the voyage of discovery, the moment you were born as a spark of divinity, during creation. Therefore, please know you have the power and knowledge and the wisdom you require to go where you will ... when you sleep, or when you close your eyes, and simply open your heart."

Once again, the meditation bell sounded right on cue … just as Swami was smiling, raising his right hand to say goodbye. What brilliant messages of guidance that Baba shares with us. They are perfect in every way. Soothing, compassionate, helpful, loving and precisely what we all need at any given moment. Thank you beloved Swami for your continued blessings and grace you bestow upon us all, and upon every form of life too.

The white feather was passed around the Circle and each devotee shared their silent contemplative experience. We closed the meeting with our usual prayer and absent healing and salutations to Sai, as always. Circle:

> *"Lokah Samastah Sukhino Bhavantu,*
> *Lokah Samastah Sukhino Bhavantu,*
> *Lokah Samastah Sukhino Bhavantu*
>
> *Shanti, Shanti, Shanti!"*

After sharing Sai's sacred ash/Vibhuti, Kate and Robert brought out the hot drinks and treats from the kitchen, and I gleefully shared the knowledge and wisdom and love, noted through my pen. Praise be to Sai/Jesus/Spirit/God. I drove home … one happy soul, indeed! Om Sai Ram/Amen.

This circle met one November. Thankfully everyone was there in plenty of time. After our hello's and a catching up with each other's news, we soon settled down for the evening's spiritual work ahead.

TRUST AND FAITH

Although Sai had left His mortal coil in 2011, it had still been Sai's 'birthday' a few days ago, and I wanted to read two lessons as a special treat for the Circle ... and for those in 'spirit' who would draw close this evening.

We all became still, and the room was soon peaceful, and quiet. Robert gave the opening prayer before we chanted the Gayathri Mantra:

> *"Aum Bhur Bhurvah Suvah*
> *Tat Savitur Varenyam*
> *Bhargo Devasya Dheemahi*
> *Dhiyo yonah Prachodayat."*

Lesson One: **HAPPY BIRTHDAY (Sai Baba)**

"Welcome to all those who will read—or hear—these words flowing through the connection to and from my heart. Right now, many of the devotee's, aspirants, and disciples of love and truth will desire to celebrate this day and night, and may even want to sing, dance, and gather in vast numbers within great halls, or in complete contrast, sit quietly contemplating upon our oneness. In doing so, you wish to honour me with the light, which emanates from inside you, so please realise I 'feel' this far beyond the bodily senses you possess.

Understand too, I recognize your thoughts, hopes and dreams, and know your soul better than you know yourself. Therefore, as you smile and uplift your love to me, I request you should also rejoice for your 'self' too. Remember, all who walk the path of true human values incorporate peace and truth into daily life, and wear the garland of divinity, which can be displayed without ego or pride.

One must comprehend I came to you via this embodiment, many years ago, and this is well documented and spoken about. Please understand though, I have walked the 'earth-plane' several times before, and have been called Saviour, Lord, Saint, and Avatar, amongst many other names. As we are one, it is important for me to do so when required. So, believe weakness will return to strength, and evil will give way to goodness across the nations and continents of the world.

You could say I am happy today, not because of your worship and devotion, but because of what you sense in me as this body of 'man', which is the reflection of your own inner heart. Appreciate that as you celebrate my return upon this annual date, in reality, the celebration is your own.

It is essential you identify and understand this, for rather than celebrating your own birthday—which then reminds you constantly of your own rebirth and the cycle of life and death—you will come to know the truth through me, and thus through yourselves. In addition, across many countries, prayers and good wishes are 'thought' or spoken, both in and from countless hearts and minds. Appreciate these resonate and resound across planes of time, space, and dimension, whilst your negative actions do the opposite, reverberating and sometimes spiralling out of control around the Earth.

I comprehend everything. Yes, the past, present, future, and all life. No one can hide from or deny the light within your hearts and souls from me. What may seem even stranger to you is the denial of one's own divinity, because at some point, every soul—upon their own journey and earthly embodiment—will question and try to understand their existence and purpose. Therefore, you must seek the truth, which lies 'inside' oneself and deep within the religions of this world.

As I have said before, I am not asking anyone to deny—or even accept under any pressure—one's heritage or culture, other than to believe in what resonates in your own heart. So, let this be true with kindness, compassion, and purity.

Of course, if you were to celebrate your life in any other way, we could deem it thoughtless, careless, and even pointless. Should this be the case, how or will your soul then feel? What would your progress and divinity be worth? Therefore, whatever you are sensing right now, do not be worried or perplexed because…

> I am the shoreline and your safe harbour.
> I am the firm and smooth ground you walk upon.
> I am the air you breathe.
> I am the Sun that warms your face.
> I am the hope of your change.
> I am the faith, which burns away doubt.
> I am the tears that melt your heart.
> I am the attainable dream of bliss.
> I am the goal of liberation,
> And I am your true desire.

So, when my physical presence no longer fills your eyes, do not fear this false absence and imaginary space, which is all a mirage. Whereas the truth, as I have stated many times, can only be revealed when the eyes of your body, soul, and mind are one.

As such, I will not fade after these few earthbound years have passed, and the legacy of my current embodiment will forever be etched upon your heart. This is a facet of your own majestic brilliance that shines brighter than the stars you witness within the firmament all around you. And, regarding this day, as many gifts and tokens of your love are laid before my lotus feet, these many thankyou notes and presents show me your true feelings. However, I return these tenfold to mark the commemoration of your own knowingness. Therefore…

> I accept your strength and your weaknesses.
> I accept your kindness and your devotion.
> I accept your pathways, which each one of you takes,
> And I accept your love and light, too.

I do not forget any of you. So, understand, while size, colour, creed, and nationality may try to divide you, you are all of one heart and sparks of divinity ... fixed upon me since time immemorial. Know that just as I walked among you in the past—and they carry my embodiment about in the present—I will always be all things to you in the future.

Now, with these joyous scenes on a wonderful day, I bear witness to this 'light' precession connecting souls across the globe, so may you find the comfort and peace you each deserve, which is your own birth right. Believe too, as you sing or pray alone, or within a gathering this day, the notes and thoughts will resonate and reflect both pitch and sound, sending your hopes and dreams beyond the physical body.

The hierarchy of light, along with the souls of your family, will shine and shed their tears of love for you all. Each tear will leave a trace of my divinity, which will become a beacon that attracts the same, to expand further than the walls where you live. Know too, this will be perceived 'inside' of you, and by those who have also opened their hearts too.

I will not deny true love, for you are the same, without difference. You cannot diminish by anything other than yourself, and so raise your 'self' to greater heights of your being. Do not restrict your spiritual education and do not feel you are less worthy than anyone or anything else. This way, you will become more than you ever thought you could be.

I empower you to express and follow your own divinity within you. You can 'walk the talk' by believing in yourself, and in turn, you will believe in me. One day, you may even sense angelic forms, which both hover and float with unimaginable grace and beauty. Appreciate they protect and guide you all, so know them in your hearts, if your eyes are yet to see. Their light and love are my gifts, forever peaceful and knowing what is right for you at all times. This present celebrates our union and your perseverance, with your continued faith and trust in yourself and in me, too.

Today, some of you believe my 'birthday' is a reminder that I am physically still with you, but millennium cannot break or ever take away the thread of my gown, which binds and links you all together and my crown of hair will forever remain in both hearts and minds. Indeed, every single soul is like a root, fixed eternally from the tree of life with my love.

Overall, this is but a fleeting day you are celebrating, and yet it is me—I AM I—who bows and kneels at your feet, to celebrate you without end. Finally, remember we are together forever, and we are all 'one'. Amen."

Lesson Two: **CELEBRATION**

"As you sit and ponder over life, you will soon realise the importance of this day, when people will gather in huge numbers around the world to celebrate the 'birthday' of an Avatar, a joyous occasion indeed. If you can truly see from the heart, then you would become delirious with happiness and peace, as the energy and vibration that flows and vibrates from an individual and the masses will encompass many cities and nations, and the radiance of 'oneness' brings wondrous feelings of being complete—without fear, anxiety or frustration.

This unique event, radiates in the same way Lord Jesus gave his sermons, and when Krishna appeared before Arjuna and his army, and upon many more events throughout your so-called history. Please understand though, even in celebration of my love—within these bodily incarnations—try to remember the true meaning of the birthday in question.

In reality, they do not specifically direct these congregations towards me, or for my benefit alone, but if they are not, then for whom? Well, the answer is easy, because this is just an annual reminder of your own rebirth into physical embodiment.

Of course, we can also say that such occasions bring together those who are 'close' to you, and this is the positive side of these gatherings, as you re-connect and link and establish yourselves as 'one' family, without realising it. Then, all must comprehend the love surrounding them, even though it is nothing more, than a reflection of the self.

Therefore, millions of souls rise and re-join their hearts to me through my embodiment of Sai Baba, whose earthly presence is 84 today. In bearing witness, what do the eyes portray to the heart … an elderly man, or Divinity that reflects and blossoms inside your own soul? Appreciate the question, because there are those who are close to this 'body', but who still cannot sense the sweet fragrance of love's purity, compassion, understanding, and patience.

In the opposite of such a circumstance, one may seem distant, living in faraway lands, but grasp the truth and light from me, through Sai's presence inside their heart or mind. Most (human) relationships, are like this. For example, two people can sit right next to each other, and yet they can be worlds apart; hearts frozen in time. Or, their feelings for one another become erased by the external behaviour … materializing through their thoughts and words and deeds.

The reverse occurs when the divinity within recognizes 'oneness' in all. Remember, distance and time hold no barriers, and are not a prison to true love—here you could think of a mother who imagines her separation from her child. Even in strenuous circumstances, where division seems to have occurred, deep down, the connection between them is never lost. On the surface, it may appear to be broken, but the link forever remains.

Justly ... so is my union with 'life' on billions of worlds and planets within countless galaxies of time and space, even though all beings and creatures outnumber—by millions of times—the combined grains of sand upon the Earth's deserts and shores. Like dot to dot upon paper, all are 'linked' as one, through so-called good or bad and dark and light.

This connection reveals your joy unto me. And so, today's celebrations in India bring smiles, singing, prayers, and thoughts of hope and faith to the forefront of so many hearts. Do not be particularly concerned though, with the trinkets of such occasions, for even golden chariots (which you think must be worthy enough to carry divinity), will eventually fade to dust.

The true seat of a soul, is inside your heart, because it cradles and protects your light and the essence of truth. It can magnify your divinity or appear as smoked glass, which obscures the precious flame from view, preventing others to feel, and know, the real you. Therefore, one must keep the host vessel clean, for like the windows of your home ... over time, one may not peer out from the inside. More importantly, the light glowing within will appear dim and often fade from sight, and subsequently anyone who draws near, will only fall foul of anger, deceit, and hate.

A soul living this way resembles a faulty lighthouse, luring passing vessels onto jagged rocks, submerging another into the waves of emotion, unleashed by the torrents of hysteria, lies, jealousy, pride, and ego. Though, please do not be dismayed—upon such an auspicious day—and do not worry or fear, because the eyes of truth are forever watching over you all.

Okay, moving on now, as it is an Avatar's birthday, would you like to give a present? And if so, would it be physical, or perhaps an emotional one instead? What do you believe you could give, right now? Remember, your pockets do not need to rattle with coin or filled with paper money, because my love is free and unconditional.

It is not vital for you to appear before my embodiment as Swami (Sai Baba) either—where you would have to travel across continents and seas—as I witness your truth through, from, and to love, in all manifestations and embodiments. This is because accents, shapes, and sizes are all exterior energy and vibration, and not your true self.

Also, wherever you reside, so do I. By seeking me, you are pursuing your own reality, and realising this will lead you forward. Appreciate, as you grow in body and mind—though not necessarily in line with your age—you will comprehend whom, what, and why you are.

If you can, try to picture the scene as banners wave gently upon the breeze, and petals fall before the elegance of divine feet, which—for those who are close by—appear to be almost floating, effortlessly, above the floor.

The sound of 'voice' will soon reverberate into song, as man, woman, girl, and boy congregate far and wide ... if only to glimpse our manifested 'purity and love'. Many hands clasp tightly together, held close to their hearts in thanks, for their prayers being answered ... while some are outstretched, willing the love and light of 'my' embodiment to be touched. A sensation and feeling of another sort of reconnection may yet be made, and of course this is a privilege, but for whom?

Well, remember your light is my light, and therefore I recognize this in your desire to be close, and so I will draw even closer to you through your trust, faith, perseverance, and love. These are the true gifts you can bestow upon me if you so wish, and in and through these you receive me too, for taking one-step towards me, I will have taken so many more to you.

Now then, as you contemplate what has been 'transcribed' from within; overcome any uncertainty from all circumstances around you. Celebrate your divinity and mine as one. Rejoice in the communion and communication that cannot fade or disappear ... one which many doubt, but never fear.

As you come to me by finding yourself, your tears may often fall. They will be tears of joy and bliss, soothing and comforting to you like a long-forgotten kiss. Please understand then, a celebration can be so precious, providing an opportunity for all to partake throughout time immemorial ... and this becomes another true reminder of our everlasting friendship and 'oneness' into eternity. Amen."

After the readings I felt quite emotional ... hiding the tears in my eyes which flowed from the well of my heart. After a brief pause, the thirty minutes silent meditation was soon underway ... signalled by the single ring of the bell. My notepad and pen were already to hand, when Sai became visible ... his majestic crown of hair materialising in my mind's eye.

"Welcome dear children of light. We are all floating and bobbing along the ocean of God's love. Know I will be the guiding light, to keep you away from the wrong shores of negativity, and deceit.

You will not flounder upon the rocks of hatred, or doubt, either. I am here. Be at peace and open your hearts."

Kimmy: "The seed of a sunflower I give to you. Your love will nourish and sustain it. Understand the flower that blooms (like your heart) will attract those souls who need guidance and reassurance. Let the light which emanates from the petals of your divine spark ignite the same truth that lies within us all. So be it. (Amen)."

Keith: "Like a metal detector, let your heart guide you to where the real golden nuggets reside. Whether in the physical world, in dream state, meditation, or upon all the dimensions of time and space and ether ... I provide you with the necessary 'tools' to reveal what you need, and when. Just have one hundred percent belief and certainty that this is the case, and everything will materialise for you at the right time."

Kate: "Just as a sunset glorifies the evening sky ... know that the same beauty and wonder resides within and around you. Reds, orange, yellows and gold are a backdrop to your divine light, which radiates beyond the impermanent world around you. The spark inside you, cascades from an never ending fountain of love and truth. Simply embrace this reality, and you will realise you are a beacon, across the universe of my heart."

Julie: "The evolution of 'man' is often called into question. The growth and expansion of your soul brings the balance to many others. This is why one can never stop learning. In addition, your heart is the key to the permeance of bliss and peace. So, never give in ... and always strive to see the truth through the eye of the body, soul and mind in unison ... as one. After all, you are the truth and truth is you, remember?"

Robert: "One's destiny does not lie, or end, with the mortal coil. You are 'spirit' ... 'spirit' is you. Your dreams enable you to quench an inner thirst, and I provide them from the well of truth. Godly dreams are real, and it's those I urge you to focus upon when recalled from a deep slumber. Your journey does not have a time limit, so forget preconceived ideas or the occasional period of doubt or concern. Understand the pillars of faith and trust will always support you in any moment or hour of need."

Swami looked around the Circle as if to survey our hearts and souls. He smiled, and I felt he was happy. His right hand became raised, and he spoke again, "Love and light to all." His beautiful radiant energy then faded, and I could no longer picture him there in the room.

Within a few seconds, the bell chimed once more, and the meditation had sadly drawn to a close. It is most strange that one can feel sad, when you experience Sai's divine love and your mind suddenly imagines a false separation and distance ... between Him, and you. However, nothing can trick the heart or keep it away from the truth. After prayers and absent healing, the mantra followed. Circle:

> *"Lokah Samastah Sukhino Bhavantu,*
> *Lokah Samastah Sukhino Bhavantu,*
> *Lokah Samastah Sukhino Bhavantu*
>
> *Shanti, Shanti, Shanti!"*

Robert shared Sai's Vibhuti, and then we passed the white feather around to discuss our experiences and/or messages. I read the transcribed notes from Swami's wonderful teachings, before cups of tea and cake. An truly amazing evening for the Circle. Thanks be to God ... and thank you forever, our beloved Swami! Om Sai Ram/Amen.

BONUS LESSON

I mentioned in the introduction (since 1996), one of the beautiful aspects of my spiritual work are the words that flow through my inner voice. I describe this as the 'In-Dweller' of my heart, in which I am co-creating with spirit, Baba, Jesus and the source of all divinity ... God. Some describe this process as channelling, inner dictation, inner dialogue or automating writing.

A more recent example of such (that I wanted to share with you), occurred after watching the late news one night, in March 2022. There were distressing images of people in physical and mental pain and anguish—whilst fleeing the bombs and devastation in Ukraine—and a great desire to hear what God would say about these events, overwhelmed me. I rushed for a notepad and pen:

A MESSAGE FROM GOD REGARDING THE WAR IN UKRAINE (5/3/22)

"You hear me before I even call, because truth and love resonate deep inside your core. It always has and always will, it's just that most people do not recognize me ... but one day all shall experience their own divinity by piercing the veil of hate and fear and anger and injustice of man versus man.

I am not blind to what occurs across—and through—the borders of your nations, whether they lie in the East or West or North and South. Such imaginary lines separate sons from mothers, daughters from fathers and cause disdain and anguish between the brotherhood of mankind,

White, black, yellow, and red are colours of skin which bring prejudices and division, when all along they bleed just the same ... and incur pain, be it physical, mental, or emotional which transcends every person. Age, sex or one's nationality and beliefs are not the prerequisites or the right to cut through one's eternal harvest of joy and peace and bliss, which is the birth right of every life and being.

During such times, it may seem a natural reaction to form opinions of right over wrong and who is to blame. Should you suppress such feelings? No, because one always needs to say what they think and act on what they speak. But again, this becomes difficult when fear for one's own safety or for their family is called into question. I do not intend to discuss karma or karmic balance in these matters but ask for each soul to remember I have given free will to express themselves from and through and to their heart.

However, the ego and the mind (which have their own attributes) often cause such devastation, whipping up a whirlwind of lies, tornadoes of grief, and oceans of tears. Homes may fall, towns and cities reduced to rubble and ash ... but evil on any scale cannot deny me and my light and love. And the same purpose and strength is within every one of you, too.

The world is beautiful. Though of course it may not seem this way when tyranny—in its many forms and guises—rears its ugly head. When electricity and gas and each form of fuel dissipates and is forcibly crushed, dismantled, or removed ... know that I am the real power to sustain your soul. Love is the greatest bond and energy in existence, so send such thoughts through the ether to touch the hearts of both kith and kin and strangers alike, no matter where they may be.

Please do not doubt me—or yourself—because this will only attempt to hinder our connection. The hungry, the thirsty, the naked, the homeless and the refugees will find this much harder to grasp or evaluate, but I implore you to simply believe. Yes, keep believing in me, for I am your true shield against seen or unseen foes ... in body or mind.

I urge you to hold on to the good both within and out ... for a new dawn is upon the horizon. The sun and 'son' will rise and shine my glory around the globe. Shadows shall disappear, as there will be nowhere for them to hide. Broken hearts, I'll mend. Smiles and laughter so quickly forgotten amidst the depths of despair will return once more. And much blood will flow away, to be cleansed by the rivers of truth, the abundance of my grace and healing from my heart.

You already have hope, though you imagine it's buried under the weight of your expectations for change ... a change of heart from those who believe they are in charge. Those in authority, in governments of false power ... harbour human traits that in reality, stem from an ivory tower.

Throughout history (and you know this), many men—with the masculine side of ego—portrayed dominance through violence or rhetoric with the flexing of physical strength and/or immature minds which sought to enslave, control, or eradicate people, towns, and cities from the face of the Earth. All have failed ...please take heart in this. Ultimately, all have to live with their actions, no matter if one is a pauper, King, Queen, religious figurehead, or a president. Do you get what I mean?

So, take just a little solace from the past, which of course you cannot change. And while 99% of life imagines that the future can't be known, because of many spiritual gifts and free will that I have bestowed upon you from the beginning of 'time', please understand you are all co-creators, and influence what has yet come to pass. In this process, I advise you that peace will overcome war and hate and anger and division.

Life always finds a way; it is who you are and why you exist to experience and to make things 'right' ... something new. Therefore, think above the clouds if they torch the sky. If a building collapses (from a so-called earthly power) into rubble and dust ... climb upon the debris to bear witness to new pastures. If home and the 'normal' way of life appears to be taken, snatched, grabbed, and pulled away from you with a vice-like grip ... do not lose heart, never lose heart because paradise and every comfort you could think of remains inside you, only a heartbeat or thought away.

Know that birds will still sing like lullabies to a child. Seeds of love fertilised in the furrows of your heart ... growing in the soil (soul) will rise to (and overcome) each challenge and reach upwards towards the light, your light, my light—our light. By empowering your own truth, you evolve—on purpose—and humanity will achieve so much more.

Therefore, please take each day as a precious gift, for no one knows if, or when, it could be their last. Each moment is an opportunity to shine or prove your real worth ... not to me, but to each other. Every human being is like a star against the backdrop of a night sky, and you can illuminate and shine as a jewel upon my crown, or stay hidden, veiled ... unable or unwilling to show the truth of you and me.

One must decide to act or simply react upon all walks of life. Will you lead and become examples of justice and fortitude or retreat inside the hardened shell of despair and not care? Know you are also divine and possess the ability to create and unify like a link in my chain of love, so demonstrate this in every thought and word and deed.

I'll leave you now to contemplate upon these words, but I remain forever your father and mother and friend ... your strength and power, through your faith in me. Amen."

And, here's a beautiful song, from Chris Eaton, to also uplift your heart and heal your soul. It's called Something New (Full ink: https://www.youtube.com/watch?v=899Q_kktrNo).

I trust that what you have just read will resonate inside you. The above lesson will also feature in the future 'part four' of the I AM I: The In-Dweller of Your Heart, series. I want you to know that you possess the same ability to listen and have your own conversations with the divine, too. Remember, only in silence can you hear your own truth. And, your inspiration, intuition, spiritual and psychic gifts are all latent within. They give you the ability to create. Only your false belief of your limitations can prevent your imagination from making the unknown 'known' and the unseen, 'seen'.

In doing so, you reveal your inner reality and become 'realised' ... in the knowledge you are already divine! This provides the basis for co-creating the life you wish to lead. You can, and will, evolve as a human being and as a soul so prepare yourself to nurture your inner child. Reach out beyond the boundary of your senses to transform the nature of your life ... and for those around you too.

When you are focused and passionate and excited about your goals and desires and 'receive' in gratitude, anything is possible. God can work through you. Do you always believe that you are the do-er, when the universe gave you the power, the fortune, the will, and the means? And God wants you to be who you were born to be. You have a place and purpose in this world, or you would not be here! I urge you to find, follow, and bask in it ... and make your dreams come true.

Queen Elizabeth II once said, "We are all visitors to this time, this place. We are just passing through. Our purpose here is to observe, to learn, to grow, to love and then we return home." This is a wonderful statement indeed, and yet it also implies a 'to and from'. How do you know that you are not already living in heaven? What if you recognised that you are already totality ... and free? You would soon evolve from all self-blame and self-sabotage and self-doubt to self-responsibility! You would act consciously not compulsively.

In essence, one must embrace change and opportunity. There is no time like the present, for 'now' is all you have. It is a gift, pre-sent from the dawn of Creation. The fact that you are reading this book indicates you have awoken from the sleep of doubt, and rather than looking back upon the imprint of your slumber—with fear or dread of a new day—you will rise with gratitude and excitement for the joy and peace and bliss it can bring.

Being compulsive in nature shall fall behind you like a dark shadow, for the way ahead is lit. The light of truth will lead you forward to living more consciously, whereby you reclaim the power within you ... and start to live a magical, purpose-filled life. Good luck!

EPILOGUE

In early 2020, the Covid pandemic hit the UK. It was with heavy hearts that this, together with Roberts poor health, were the main contributing factors for the Sai Baba Peterborough Circle having to close.

After all these years, I am so pleased to now share my story of our extraordinary meetings ... whereby Sai walked amongst us, and spoke and blessed us all beyond compare. He was, and is, and always will be, connected to our hearts ... for he is the Divine, who forever forms the Circle of trust and hope and friendship.

However, regardless of where you search for truth, be this with a spirit 'guide' or teacher ... a guru, in one's faith and/or religion ... a soul needs to connect with their own divinity and go beyond the boundary of their senses. We achieve this through our heart's centre, where our love and power reside and resonate inside.

In addition, Swami often said, "It is through service that man can expect to redeem his life. He is not a human at all who has no compassion and love in 'him'. The path to self-realization is through love and service."

Remember, the Divine, Source/God shall always be your guide and confidante as you continue your Earth-plane sojourn.

Love and light and peace to one and all, David.

FURTHER READING

You will find your own guidance and inspiration every day, week, month, or year as nothing in life is ever by 'chance'. You will always be directed to what is most appropriate for your needs at that time, helping you to find inner peace and balance, as well as your own spiritual education, growth and understanding. Here is a selection of my favourite books and authors, which I hope you will enjoy reading too. Good luck!

Sai Baba Gita-
The Way to Self-Realization and Liberation in this age.
By Al Drucker
ISBN 0-9638449-0-3

Conversations with God
By Neale Donald Walsh
Book 1 - ISBN 0-340-69325-8
Book 2 - ISBN 0-340-76544-5
Book 3 - ISBN 0-340-76545-3

The Message of a Master
By John McDonald
ISBN 0-931432-95-2

The Celestine Prophecy-An Adventure
By James Redfield
ISBN 0-533-40902-6

Anastasia- The Ringing Cedar series -Book 1
By Vladimir Megre
ISBN 978-0-9801812-0-3

A Course in Miracles
By The Foundation for Inner Peace
ISBN 0-670-86975-9

The Winds of Change
By Stephanie J. King
ISBN 978-0954242169

The Day my life changed
By Carmel Reilly
ISBN 978-1-84509-420-1

Confessions of a Pilgrim
Bu Paulo Coelho
ISBN 0-7225-3293-8

A Mind of your Own
By Betty Shine
ISBN 0-00-255894-7

Angel Inspiration
By Diana Cooper
ISBN 0-340-73323-3

Chicken Soup for the Soul
By Jack Canfield and Mark Victor Hansen
ISBN 0-09185-428-8

The Complete Book of Dreams
By Edwin Raphael
ISBN 0-572-01714-6

The Bible Code
By Michael Drosnin
ISBN 0-297-82994-7

The Secret
By Rhonda Byrne
ISBN: 978-1847370297

Noah Finn & the Art of Suicide
By E. Rachael Hardcastle
ISBN: 978-1999968816

Noah Finn & the Art of Conception
By E. Rachael Hardcastle
ISBN: 978-1999968861

Evolving on Purpose
By Soulful Valley Publishing
ISBN: 978-1739993603

Lessons from the Source: A Spiritual Guidebook for Navi- gating Life's Journey
By Jack Armstrong
ISBN 0-615-86984-X

How Sai Baba Attracts Without Direct Contact–Diary of a 21st Century Devotee
By Dr Tommy. S.W. Wong
ISBN 1-4486-0416-8

Signposts
By Denise Linn
ISBN 0-7126-749-7

Universe Has Your Back: Transform Fear to Faith
By Gabrielle Bernstein
ISBN 1-4019-4654-8

THINK and RECEIVE MIRACLES
By Lalitha Donatella Riback
ASIN: B0D489359G

SOUTHFUL POEMS
By Soulful Valley Publishing
ASIN: B0CNWYGX9W

Enlightenment Codes for Cosmic Ascension
By Sabrina Di Nitto
ISBN: 978-9464517309

ACKNOWLEDGEMENTS

To my wife Caroline for all her love, support, and encouragement ... and for all those of love and light and truth who have connected through my speaking heart.

ABOUT THE AUTHOR

David is a multiple Amazon International bestseller and has helped to conduct spiritual development and healing circles for over 25 years. He has also been a guest speaker—sharing his enlightened experiences to promote 'oneness'—at various Mind, Body, and Spirit engagements in the UK.

Through inner-dictation, dream interpretation, meditation, mindfulness, precognition, and healing ... the books he co-writes with 'Spirit' provide you with the foundation to discover your own path of truth. With a renewed sense of purpose, the spiritual guidance and education you receive, can help you reach the goal of self-realization and bliss—within the permanence of love and light. David is tee-total and a vegetarian who loves the sunshine, nature, animals, and his wife!

ALSO BY DAVID KNIGHT

Pathway

Deliverance of Love, Light and Truth

I Am I: The Indweller of Your Heart—Book One

I Am I: The Indweller of Your Heart—Book Two

I Am I: The Indweller of Your Heart—Book Three

I Am I: The Indweller of Your Heart— Collection

Leave the Body Behind—Sojourns of the Soul

A Pocket Full of God

Rhyme & Reason

FORESIGHT

INVITATION/FREE EBOOK

If you enjoyed reading, UNITY of FAITHS—The Circle of Trust and Hope and Friendship ... download *Deliverance of Love, Light, and Truth* for free when you join David›s mission for ‹full and blissful life›.

To learn more, visit https//www. AscensionForYou.com

GLOSSARY &
SPIRITUAL REFERENCE GUIDE

Abundance: Awaken your consciousness, to the knowingness of your own creative abundant energy, a part of creation.

Affirmations: Help us to purify our thoughts and restructure the dynamic of our brains. Personal affirmations are positive, specific sentences which need to be in the present tense, often repeated several times to encourage or motivate yourself. The word affirmation comes from Latin 'affimare', originally meaning "to make steady, strengthen."

Amen: A Hebrew word that means "so be it". Usually said at the end of a prayer, we are asking God, "Please let it be as we have prayed". NB. When people place their hands/palms together it signifies a negative and positive flow of energy. The left receives and the right sends. The same hand gesture is a customary Hindu and Buddhist greeting called Namaste but is also used when leave-taking too. It is sometimes spoken as Namaskar or Namaskaram.

Angel: The word "angel" is derived from the Greek word Angelos which means 'messenger'. They are divine spirits, each of God's consciousness and these beings of light intercede for us, answering our prayers and calls for help. In Hinduism, they are called devas or devis. In Islam, a belief in Angels who materialise out of light and function as Allah's messengers is one of the six pillars of faith.

Archangel: Hierarchs (leaders) of the Angels.

Ascension: Is the process whereby the soul, (having balanced / removed karma and fulfilled its divine plan) merges first with the universal/Christ consciousness and then with the living presence of the I AM THAT I AM. Once the Ascension has taken place, the soul becomes a permanent atom of the 'Body of God'. Please remember, your ascension is not something you plan for or takes place on a certain date. You are actively choosing a process to evolve into higher consciousness ... through expanded awareness and integrating the higher reverberation of your spiritual self. So, the act of ascending; is to climb to a greater plane/dimension which involves total transformation on all levels (all that you are) ... realigned with divine love. In Christian belief, the ascent of Jesus Christ into Heaven on the 40th day after his resurrection ... his return to sit on the right-hand side of the 'Father'.

Anamnesis: Knowledge through remembering ...what we know on the level of the mind or spirit before we descend into a body.

Ashram: Hermitage: a residence for spiritual aspirants and saints.

Atma: The real Self, one's divinity, God, the substance of everything, the spark of God within which is the true Self. The Atma does not contradict the doctrines of any faith.

Aum: (Also see OM) This is the universal, sacred, and indestructible sound. The frequency of the same word that went forth as the origin of creation ... the basis and root of all sounds of your existence. By sounding the AUM comes our oneness and can provide many benefits to the body and mind. It is a spiritual process unaffected by culture or language and is the pathway to how your energies function. Each letter stands for a component of our divinity and is intended to be sounded separately ... with repetition and great awareness as the reverberation flows within you, moving from the navel to the tip of your nose. (Remember to pronounce the letters as Aa's, Ooo's and Mmm's). The A comes forth from Alpha (our Father) as the initiator, the creator, the beginning of consciousness of being ... the thrust of power. The M is the is the OM (our Mother) the conclusion/ending ... one with the Holy Spirit—therefore the positive and negative polarities of being are pronounced. From the A to the Om, all the vastness of creation is contained and so the U in the centre is the cup cradling you (the centre piece)—the real self in universal manifestation—so, A-U-M is the Trinity in unity. In the East, Hindus refer to the Trinity as Brahma, Vishnu, and Shiva ... the relevant forces of Creation, Maintenance and Destruction. In the West... the Trinity is Father, Son, and the Holy Spirit. NB. The meaning in Sanskrit is "I bow, I agree, I accept". I bow before God Almighty, I agree that I am the 'son', and I accept my immortal destiny.

Automatic writing: A type of divination where the pen appears to direct the writer instead of the writer directing the pen. In a paranormal sense, automatic writing is synonymous with autography, psychography and spirit writing. Some who experience this phenomenon have also written in other languages which they do not even speak! So, with pen in hand, the writer basically sits back, clears his mind, and waits for the pen, which appears to take on a life of its own. Although autography—meaning in one's own handwriting—is the least accurate synonym for automatic writing. In addition, spiritualists believe that automatic writing is a form of spirit 'contact' with the living; hence the name 'spirit writing'. Others also believe that automatic writing is the elimination of mental censorship and the ability to tap the thoughts of the unconscious mind (psychography).

Avatar: An incarnation of God taking a form according to the age in which the incarnation occurs. Descent of God on Earth.

Awareness: Is vital to your progress as a seeker to connect with your divine nature. Therefore, you must become aware of the external chatter which detracts from your inner enquiry. Do not just 'observe' but give your full attention to your consciousness—not the body and mind. And it will help if you only focus on one activity at a time ... so do not multitask. This way, divinity will manifest through you! Remember, the less you do, the less personality is involved and the more 'aware' of life you become.

Balance: We know that karma is action, and all your experiences of joy, misery, happiness, and suffering happen within you. Once you have truly grasped the fact that this encompasses your entire system of mind, body, soul, and energy, it can be the springboard to finding true balance. This becomes easier if you don't let the mind work against you ... a necessity to experience the divinity and bring brilliance into your life. So, try to attain this through every aspect your physicality, your diet, thoughts, sleep, posture and breathing ... everything!

Bhagavad Gita: A principle Indian Scripture ... the Song of God.

Bhagawan: "Bhaga" means 'the One who is the repository of all Divine attributes and is uniquely worthy of adoration. "Ga" refers to 'One who has all the excellences and who creates, sustains and reabsorbs everything'. The letter "Bha" has two meanings ... Sambharta and Bharta. Sambharta means, 'One who is competent to make Nature the instrument of the creative process because He is also competent to sustain what is created, He is called Bharta. "Bha" has other meanings as Shanti (peace), light, effulgence, and illumination. "Ga" means 'all persuasive'. "Van" (Vanthudu in Telugu) means 'One who is capable'. Hence the term Bhagawan means 'the One who is capable of lighting the Divine effulgence, illuminating wisdom and is the Eternal Inner Light of the Soul@. Can there be anything greater than earning the love of such an omniscient and omnipotent Lord? There is nothing on Earth or beyond it which is equal to Divine Love. To make all endeavour to earn that love is the whole purpose and meaning of human existence. (Divine discourse, Jan 14, 1998)

Bhajan: Devotional song; a song of adoration of God.

Bhakthi: Devotion.

Bliss/blissful: This is not a goal or attainment in itself. You need to make it your purpose, the foundation and way of your life. Everything else plays out from this. To experience true bliss one must have both divine grace and human endeavour. Baba used to explain this by using a simple analogy regarding the breeze from a fan ... you cannot experience the breeze without the fan or the electrical energy. He urges us to improve ourselves ... to become better human beings and make our lives sublime.

Body: The vessel (some call it a shell, overcoat, or even a bubble) which houses our senses through which we perceive everything. The physical body is also shaped by our evolutionary and genetic memory. It thrives or withers by the food we eat, inherited from Mother Earth, and nourished by creation. In addition, it allows the faith and goodwill of the divine intent.

Bondage: What we have created for ourselves materialises from nothing more than our likes and dislikes. Bondage also refers to the identification we have placed upon our bodies and minds, and not with people, places, or material/physical objects. It all lies in your mind ... your thoughts. One who considers themselves free becomes free. One who considers themselves bound remains bound. So, you are what you think and therefore if you think you are just body and mind you are ... if you think you are boundless you are!

Ironically, use your thoughts to go beyond the bondage of your thoughts! Remember, there is no bondage in consciousness.

Causal body: The highest and innermost 'body' which veils the Atma/soul. A doorway to higher consciousness.

Chakras: The Chakra 'system' is a vital part of our mental, emotional, physical, and spiritual 'bodies'. There are 112 funnel-shaped energy points within… and 2 'outside' of us.

Clairaudience: Claire means "clear" in French and means clear 'hearing'. It is the psychic ability to hear voices, sounds, and messages from beyond the physical world. Psychics who are clairaudient hear voices, sounds or music that are not audible to the normal ear. They receive these messages mentally or within their ears. Possessing this skill may provide you with a clear path of communication between yourself and higher spirits or beings.

Compassion: A frequency of divine love coming from the soul through the heart chakra.

Consciousness: Intellect without memory … pure and unsullied by the mind's impressions and body experiences.

Darshan: Sight of a Holy person. In Prashanti Nilayan (In Sri Sathya Sai's main *ashram, darshan* usually took place twice a day. Sai Baba would walk amongst the crowds, talking and taking letters from devotees).

Death: The important aspect here is that you must experience to 'know'. Therefore, one has to acknowledge what you do or do not know, and what you believe or disbelieve too. Death is fiction, death is life, death is a continuation. When the body dies it has become unsustainable for life (your soul), so the conscious mind moves on, retaining all qualities bar discrimination. We need to relate this to karma yet again, for it acts like a bubble retaining the soul within the body. Imagine the bubble has burst and the air within now merges with totality, and so becomes enlightened.

Decrees: Relate to the science of the spoken word. A step up from all prayer forms both East and West, they combine prayer, meditation, and visualisation, and place a special emphasis on affirmations using the name of God—I AM THAT I AM. An effective method in balancing karma, spiritual resolution, and soul advancement.

Desire: Is the force ... the current of 'life'

Destiny: Of every human being is to return to the source from which he came. People often blame a negative outcome as a result of their so-called destiny, but in doing so they place a total limitation upon their life and so cannot be free. However, it is you (and only you) who makes your life! We could also define destiny as what you create for yourself.

Devotion: All forms of devotion arise from your emotions. It provides you with a sense of freedom and comes from the heart... unlike belief, which materialises from the mind. It is what is devoid of 'you' ... and allows grace to flow through you. One may experience this by allowing a greater intelligence to work through you whilst keeping your intellect at bay.

Divine guidance: When you become 'still' within the silence of your heart, (Baba would recommend ten to fifteen minutes) ... pose your question. When the mind has become clear, your doubts and confusion will be resolved which allows you to move forward with conviction.

Divinity: The state or quality of being divine.

Dharma: Right action, truth in action, righteousness, morality, virtue, duty, the dictates of God, code of conduct.

Earth-plane: The world of material form.

East and West: East is often related to the destruction of all that is unreal... and the purification of the veil of Maya (illusion) by Lord Shiva. West is usually termed with the action of the Holy Spirit.

Ego: The ego is the unconscious/lower self, and it only identifies with the body and mind. However, in truth this lower self does not really exist ... it is only an absence of awareness, just like darkness which is the absence of light. So, one cannot be aware of and also ecstatic/blissful at the same time. In contrast, your reality is the infinite or higher self ... pure intelligence. Remember, you do not need to 'see' to identify with the 'all knowing' ... and when you remove the ego you are able to experience pure joy.

Enlightenment: Everything is lit up; you see the reality of life/existence. True insight and comprehension.

Etheric Body: This is the body charged by God with the Holy memory of all things lovely and beautiful within the substance of the divine world ... in order that you may bask in that power which one day you will know to its fullest.

Experience: Only by turning inward can you discover bliss and liberation and true peace of the divine. You must experience it yourself, and this will not happen by reading a book, traveling somewhere, or when you listen to any other human being.

Fate: Fate is the real debate. Could it be when you fail to create your own destiny? Try to imagine you were about to run a race ... you know there's a finishing line, but you do not what is going to happen between the start and finish.

Forbearance: An important quality indeed. The spiritual seeker must appreciate that happiness in their life occurs by totally trusting in the universe and remaining in an acceptance mode. This way, one's joy and peace will always remain undisturbed, and you will never feel frustrated, impatient, or let down.

Forgiveness: Is the key to connect with the open door of your own 'Christ-self'. The quality of love is all-encompassing and all-forgiving. Learn to forgive others and most of all yourself, for true healing.

Free will: The discretion to use or not use ... the freedom of 'choice'. The question then arises over how much of your life unfolds automatically or compulsively (if it is not happening the way you want it to) rather than acting with your intelligence ... consciously. In addition, free will was not granted or given power by any governing body or power, other than whim and what you (and God) already are. For such a reason, all your reaction to action, and your cause to the effect can be nothing more than this. Therefore, as you make your way along the journey that we call life ... you—as a soul—can shine as a billion suns, or as a dim light covered by a blanket of hate and doubt.

Glory: Recognise the glory of your own soul, your divine link with the glory of God, creator, universal intelligence. See and feel its glorious reflection within yourself.

Gaythri Mantra: A mantra that invokes the supreme intelligence to illumine the intellect and remove ignorance.

God: Is the only reality in every person ... everything else is transient . God is the substratum, the reality of everything, and the only permanent aspect of 'man'. Unlimited by time or space and undefinable by name or forms. Remember, there is no God superior to yourself. Swami has said, "If you think you are small you will continue to be small. Therefore, think 'I AM GOD. This truth will bestow on you the Divine aspect which you should contemplate upon." SSIB 1993.

Grace: Receiving God's grace can be automatic, but usually follows the effort and endeavour made by the 'seeker'. It requires non-resistance and unconditional acceptance in the reality of our oneness and boundless state. Know that even your so-called 'troubles; you may experience are the gifts of the Divine. When you surrender all of your actions, you will surely receive His grace.

Guru: 'Gu' means darkness, 'ru' means dispeller. Therefore, a Guru is someone who dispels darkness ... to throw light on your very nature of existence. A teacher; preceptor; a guide to spiritual liberation.

Happiness: To be happy you must stop finding fault with anything and everything ... situations, people, and things. One must surrender to the acceptance of what is because true happiness has no cause behind it. To experience this, you must know yourself by removing all dependence on external situations ... which allows you to discover the true 'uncaused' happiness of your real nature—bliss.

Healing: Is a letting-go process... do it every day as you hold and welcome love into your heart. Every day you have the power to express the light of your divinity to any life who needs it. Know that the healing process takes place first in the soul—spiritually and emotionally. Then the mind, mentally and visually ... followed by the body, which will always reflect the state of your true and higher self.

Heart: Your heart is a gift from creation. It is the seat of your soul and the very altar of God. Comprehend that inside the heart there is a central chamber, surrounded and protected by a forcefield known as the 'cosmic interval'. This chamber is separated from Matter, and no microscope or probing can ever discover it. Only true vision— when the eyes of the body, soul and mind are in unison can one bear witness to its magnificence. Know that it is the connecting point of the powerful crystal cord of light that descends from your God presence—which sustains the beating of your physical heart. This also gives your life purpose and a reason for integration with the cosmos. Therefore, we must cherish this contact point of 'life' by turning within to pay conscious recognition to it.

Hierarchy of Light: The cosmic Hierarchy is a 'universal chain' of individualized God free beings fulfilling attributes and aspects of God's infinite Selfhood.

Higher Self: A person's spiritual self, their true identity … a focus to many meditation techniques, as opposed to the physical body.

Human being: A definition which defines us. Our consciousness and intellect distinguish us from all other life forms because we know 'how to be'.

I: Most people—when saying 'I'—are referring to (or thinking of) their body or mind, however 'I' represents our 'Immortal consciousness'.

I AM: You are saying "God in me is" … so that everything you say after these words manifests in our world.

I AM THAT I AM: The name and living presence of 'God' the 'as above so below'. In the West—the path of the Mother—descends. In the East, "OM TAT SAT OM"—the path of the Spirit—ascends. The energy of your being and all that is locked in imperfection becomes a spiral of the ascension and returns to the heart of the God presence.

Identity: Your true identity is part of the cosmos. You have to shift from what the mind believes is just the physical, to that of consciousness. Without the light, your identity is like a moth drawn to—and darting around— the flame of truth … but charring or burning your wings to depart into the abyss of suffering and darkness … without having attained illumination and liberation.

Immortality: Those of faith and religious persuasion believe the indefinite continuation of a person's existence, even after death. Other opinions state that mental activity is nothing but cerebral activity and as such ... death brings the total end of a person's existence. In truth, immortality is the fruit of sacrifice.

Inspiration: One of the greatest gifts of your divinity is to become the example, the inspiration whereby you move from 'unwillingness' to 'willingness'. God provides you with droplets of truth, those golden nuggets of wisdom, the fragments of creation to stimulate your thoughts and actions to 'create'. Even if you feel that you have not reached the pinnacle, or conversely feel like you have plummeted to the depths ... you retain the ability inside you to inspire

Intention: The idea that is conveyed or intended to be conveyed to the mind by, symbols, language, or action. Intentions keep you in the moment, the aim or purpose for doing what you are doing. When you set an intention, you are determining to act in a certain way. Before setting an intention, it is best to pause and reflect about your what you really need. Perhaps its self-love, being more compassionate towards yourself, or nurturing your inner child? Try to focus an intention to what best meets your needs right now. You can use an intention to be a reminder of how you want to live each day, but in essence they are about how you feel when you do something.

Invocation: The act or instance of invoking, a prayer or command to a higher power, deity, spirit, God for assistance, divine guidance, forgiveness, and protection. Sometimes used in the opening of a religious festival. It is also a way of bringing the best out in you.

Jiva: The individual soul that resides in the body.

Journey: The most important journey you can undertake in this lifetime is from being unconscious to conscious. This includes your thoughts, words and deeds and everything within and around you!

Joy: Try to bring a feeling of lightness to your heart and a renewed joy in living. Laughter and joyous love will bring out the child in you, transmuting any feelings of negativity and heaviness within you. Make your days joyful and watch the world around change for the better! In reality, your true accomplishment is the joy you cause in the 'heart' of God ... and 'joy' derived from service reacts upon the 'body' and helps to keep you free from disease too.

Kali Yuga: An age of egoism and self-interest resulting in jealousy, fear, greed and hatred.

Kama: Desire; lust.

Karma: Literally means 'Action' (activity/work/duty) and is of your own making. Most of your actions are unconscious, played out through one's physical, mental, emotional and life-energy. Also believed to be the totality of a person's actions and conduct and memory during successive incarnations or regarded as cause and effect that may influence their destiny. Karma is also considered to be a law or principle through which such influence is believed to operate ... fate resulting from one's previous actions. However, counteracting a 'fate/destiny' scenario, it is incredibly empowering to know that each day is our own making. Misery or joy are the choice which affects the very nature of our lives. Therefore, you are responsible for your own future ... it is in your own hands!

Leela: Divine sport, play or a miracle of the Lord.

Lingham: An ellipsoid-shaped stone worshipped as the symbol of creation.

Light: The highest frequency we know. Your physical eyes can only see that which is stopped by light. However, the pure element of the 'I' bears witness to all creation because it sees without being tarnished by memory, and views everything exactly the way it is. Jesus once said, "The light of the body is eye (I). If therefore thine eye (I) be single, thy whole body shall be full of light."

Love: Love is the way you are. Love enables us to fulfil the destiny of the soul in conscious outer manifestation—a just and merciful compassion that is always rewarded by individual creative fulfilment. Through the power of love, man learns how they may impart into others the beauty and compassion that they have received from God. Love does not need to have sustenance from anyone, therefore, if you are loving … it spreads!

Maha Yogi: Sage of the highest order.

Mandir: Temple.

Manifesting: Bringing your desires and aspirations into being … through focusing your thoughts and energy and passion. The manifestation process is the transmutation of thought into the physical world. It can help you bring into real life the things you want, whether that is love, improved health, money etc. It is important to note that is not so much about getting, but more about becoming. In essence, when you let go of the lack, you become abundant. Likewise, when you give … so shall you receive. Note that manifestation's origins stem from spirituality and religion, because if something spiritual transcends into reality, it is said to be a manifestation. Remember, keep using your imagination. Then, through joyful visualization and words of deep desire … you'll just need to believe and keep receptive!

Mantra: Sacred syllable or word(s) to be repeated (often silently) for attaining perfection or Self-realization; a mystic formula for spiritual enlightenment. A word or formula (often in Sanskrit). They attune you and govern the release or attraction of life-energy, which becomes deposited in your aura. This expands over time, gaining momentum. For example, this powerful mantra from India "OM NANORA RIJA NIYA" tunes oneself with the infinite. "O infinite God, I want your will to be done in me".

Maya: The illusion of seeing the unreal as real, of mistaking the transient for the eternal. The cosmic illusion whereby the 'Truth' is revealed.

Meditation: Practiced for millennia, and originally intended to develop spiritual understanding, awareness, and direct experience of ultimate reality. Although an important spiritual practice in many religions and traditions, it can be practiced regardless of someone's religious or cultural background. It can be used with other forms of medical treatment, and as a complementary therapy for the many stress-related conditions. Types of meditation include concentration, movement, mindfulness, and transcendental. When you meditate you are just withdrawing support from your personality, you are creating a distance between your true self and your mind ... in essence, observing from an elevated, clearer viewpoint. In fact, the true state of meditation is wherever and whenever you place yourself in touch with God! (So, try to think of God and love God from the moment you awake, to the time you go to sleep. Keeping you mind, your attention always on God).

Moha: Liberation.

Mind: Eastern philosophy and wisdom state there are 16 segments to the mind. The 4 main 'parts' relate to intellect, identity, memory (evolutionary and genetic) and pure intelligence. It encapsulates our thoughts and emotions. NB. People often refer to their 'monkey' mind during meditation, but our purpose is to liberate it, not control it!

Mind Fasting: Bracketing any distracting or disturbing thoughts aside so we can 'fast' from thinking about them while we listen to God. (See also Silence and Stillness).

Mindfulness: Reconnecting with our bodies, and the sensations they experience. Becoming aware of our thoughts and feelings through our senses—knowing what is going on inside and around ourselves—at any given moment.

Nirvana: The state of union with God with the mind in perfect balance, unaffected by experiences whether good or bad.

Om: (Also see Aum) The basic primeval sound (vital vibration) from which all comes.

Omnipotent: Having unlimited or Universal power, authority, or force; all-powerful.

Omnipresent: The state of being everywhere at once. All-pervading, Universal, ever-present.

Omniscient: Having total knowledge, knowing everything. All-knowing, all-seeing, wise.

Omkar: Repetition of *Om*.

Path: It does not matter what route you take if you are just constantly striving for 'more'. Know that you will never reach the destination if you continually require and crave more love, more money, more success etcetera. Only the pathless path brings you the perception, the clarity and the focus needed to liberate and experience perpetual bliss.

Patience: Recognise and feel the principle of patience to release tension in the mind and body and your life. With greater awareness, an increase in your level of endurance and ability to suffer restlessness and annoyance without complaint.

Personality: This is the one and the only real difference between each human being. It reflects and manifests as our likes and dislikes in every way and form imaginable ... and thus induces bondage.

Prasad: Food offered to God and then eaten by devotees.

Prema: The highest form of pure love ... the very breath of life.

Purification: A high dimensional frequency which can operate at a causal body level throughout the subtle bodies (mind, etheric, physical, and emotional), and the auric field. This transmutes lower energies and allows a new feeling of purity to filter through the conscious mind.

Responsibility: One could say this is our ability to respond to everything that occurs within and outside of us. In real terms, our ability to respond to any given situation is limitless, whereas our ability to act is limited. It is the simplest way to express our divinity too.

Sathya: Truth.

Sathya Sai Baba: Sai Baba incarnated in this age first a Shirdi Sai Baba ... who left His body in 1918. Eight years later, on 23 November 1926, Sathya Sai Baba was born. He then left his mortal coil in 2011. His third incarnation will be born as Prema Sai Baba.

Self-realization: The expression used in psychology, spirituality, and Eastern religions. Can be defined as the fulfilment by oneself of the possibilities of one's character, personality, potential, and Divinity. To become 'realised' means you finally perceive what is already there! Please note ... that the instruments of your perception are all outward bound, but the seat of experience is within you.

Senses: Nature has allowed you to live life through the sense organs. Eyes provide sight to beautiful scenes and all your surroundings. Ears enable sound and melody to soothe or stir your emotions. The nose permits the aroma and fragrances of creation to ignite your imagination. Taste enables you to savour nutritious food which give life and health to the body. Touch gives you the opportunity to know and feel personal contact. However, the common theme with each sense is that they all crave and desire … which only leads to your likes and dislikes creating bondage. You must, therefore, use your intelligence to control the mind and take charge of the senses for spiritual life …and make them your servants and not your masters! A true seeker will only become fulfilled this way to experience eternal bliss. N.B. An old Indian metaphor captures this perfectly, "Use the intellect-charioteer to take charge of the reins of the mind and your sense-horses … if you want to reach the destination of Self-realization."

Seva: Selfless service.

Shanti: Peace.

Shakthi: Divine energy.

Shiva: The Destroyer in the trinity of Brahma (the Creator), Vishnu (the Preserver), and Shiva.

Silence: Is that which is NOT the basis of sound. Keeping silent has an immensely powerful impact on your life … a representation of 'nothingness'. Many guides also state you should reduce what you say by 50% … and even my wife says I talk too much! Remember, silence is the speech of the spiritual seeker.

Signs: One may deem 'signs' as a spiritual language. What I am referring to is the imagery, symbols, sounds or any information that comes from our spirit guides who watch over us all ... forms of communication as it were. Spirit will use any means at their disposal to convey what you are meant to hear, see, or feel. Some call this assistance from the 'other' side ... heaven if you like. One of my own favourite examples of this occurred when I was leaving a job in financial services—which in the end I started to loathe. It was a very stressful time after going through much personal upheaval and loss. I was about to drive away from the office for the last time. The sun was shining in a clear blue sky. I opened the car window and took a deep sigh of breath. Turning on the car radio, a chorus of a song by Ultra Nate bellowed out ... 'Cause you're free, to do what you want to do. You've got to live your life, do want you want to do.' There are many 'signs' you may know of, like a white feather falling at your feet or even smelling the perfume or aftershave of a loved one who has crossed over. These are but gentle, wonderful reminders that we are all watched over and loved. Remember everything is energy/God. And love is the most powerful force in creation. If you are ever in doubt over your divine connection with a loved one ... think of an object, an image, a place or even a feeling that connects you both. Something simple would suffice. Ask the universe for a sign and it will come. Allow the universe to work through you with an open mind and heart, and it will speak back—just be ready to receive it!

Sojourn: A temporary stay; a brief period of residence.

Soul: The soul is not the object of intellect ...but the very source of your intellect!

Spirit world: Is real, but not always innocent. This is why whenever you are in contact with the 'other side', it is important to question who and what they are. Clarify their purpose. They will not mind if they are genuine and loving. According to Scripture, those spirits that are not the Holy Spirit or angels are evil spirit. On rare occasions, I have been privileged (during dream state) to assist in spirit rescue work. This involves venturing into deep darkness and helping to raise another 'soul' towards their reality ... 'light'.

Spiritual Healing: Spiritual healing has been a principle of Spiritualism since its establishment as a religion. However, it differs from faith healing in that the patient need have no faith in the treatment. Faith healers also claim instant cures, while in Spiritual healing the cures are rarely instantaneous. In addition, rather than belief in divine intervention, the Spiritual healer believes that spirits work through him or her to energize and heal the patient. Over the years I have been blessed to work for 'spirit' this way. This privilege is a gift that I believe we all possess, and I always found that when healing flowed through me, the recipient could either feel warmth or even coolness ... depending on the condition that was being treated. Some describe the energy that comes through as like a sticky candyfloss feeling. I would always ground myself as it would feel like negativity ... blackness which would then flow back through my arms. On a friend who was about to leave their mortal coil, I nearly puked up ... it was so 'bad' that I almost passed out. Basically, healing is love from spirit, through spirit and to spirit for our emotional, mental, and physical 'bodies' we possess.

Spiritual seeker: Many people understand that being a seeker involves making a total and absolute surrender to 'life' by accepting whatever comes their way. However, when transformation, guidance, and the materialisation of what is sought does not occur ... grave doubt may arise. Then, further obstacles or suffering will usually generate the question, "Why me?" or "Why is it happening?" But this only creates a further barrier, so it is crucial not to think or ask the 'why' question! If you can only transcend the need for any clarification in all your experiences (whether deemed 'good', 'bad', or indifferent) this will finally allow the Universal consciousness and life-energy to resolve the situation for your higher good and at the earliest opportunity too.

Spiritualism: The three main aspects are ... the survival of the spirit after death, the ongoing concern of the deceased (spirits) for the living, and also the ability of those spirits to communicate with the living through a medium (a person who serves as an intermediary between the spirits and the living).

Spirituality: Going beyond the boundary of the body/senses. You experience the reality past the physical presence, and in life, react with your intelligence consciously. In essence, spiritual life is transformation!

Spiritual Life: Is simply merging with God.

Stillness: Being still empowers you because it allows you to be in touch with another dimension. When you are consciously 'still', the energy you access becomes a link between the non-physical and physical elements of your existence ... so you are able to witness the reality of life in its entirety. In essence, you leave your perception of a limited identity behind to see and experience the truth. Understand that stillness is not sleep, which is unconscious slumber.

Time: Is the only proof of the existence of 'matter', however, seconds, minutes and hours are not your true pillars of creation. It is not how little or how much time you have, but what you do with it that counts. When you are joyful, time will seem to disappear, when you are miserable ... a day can feel like eternity. When you turn inward and have no sense of body, you detach yourself from the clock face and the unreal develops into reality. When you truly accept the awareness and the inevitability of the 'moment', all suffering is gone. Understand everything in creation is in this moment, whereas your mind thinks of the future (imagination) and the past (memory). So, one must be conscious and live in the moment, for it is only this moment which is inevitable!

Transformation: Nothing of the old 'you' should remain—in contrast to improvement, which is just a 'change.' As such, the object of your desires may alter your destination, but only when you stop seeking/asking/striving for what you do not have can you change the inner process of one's life. By transformation, you shift oneself to a completely new dimension of perception and experience … hence 'self-transformation'.

Tranquillity: When the subtle vibrations which surround the body become disturbed, you feel stressed. You need to combat this, so take the mind elsewhere. Visualise somewhere calm, perhaps by a still lake or a special place held dear to your heart. Allow peace to wash over you and bring tranquillity to your body, thoughts, and consciousness.

Truth: Can only be perceived and experienced, it cannot be interpreted. It should be treated as life giving as breath itself … nothing more precious or sweeter or more lasting.

Turning inward: When you sit still in silence, there is an opportunity to 'experience' your reality beyond the senses. In doing so, what you have previously classed as your identity (which were bound by one's sex, race, religion, and beliefs), will break free and lose its limitations.

Unconditional love: This form of love is not emotional and has no strings or ties. It is the only true healing power, so try to allow your heart to be activated in this way.

Unity: Is divinity.

Via Negativa: The path of 'with outness' ... that theologians state that when all 'imagined' supports are removed, you will 'know thyself'.

Vibhuti: Sacred/Holy ash of cow dung. Baba would shower this ash from His forehead, His palm, His feet and His pictures. It is symbolic of the ultimate divine reality which remains when the ego is burned away by the fire of illumination and enlightenment. For devotees, this gift of ash (sacred prasad), is the cure for all sickness, whether mental, emotional, spiritual or physical.

Vibration and energy: The resonance of your true 'self'. We are all at different stages of spiritual development, so the intensity of reverberation (sound) within would indicate the energy level you have reached. Every substance has its own frequency, its own keynote. Every sound has form, and every form has sound.

Visualisation: A mental image, like one's visual perception.

Vedas: Hindu scriptures; the entire sacred revelations of truth, chief among them are four books ... the *Rigveda,* the *Samaveda*, the *Atharvaveda* and the *Yajurveda*.

Wisdom: 'Wise dominion' ... wisdom to nourish the mind—for illumination and the right use of the knowledge of Universal law.

Words: On this journey called 'life' it is important to live in truth, so try speaking what you feel and act what you speak. Sai once said, "That words can plunge you into prison, or release you into freedom."

Yoga: A group of physical, mental, and spiritual practices or disciplines which originated in ancient India. One of six Astika schools of Hindu philosophical traditions. In the West, it is often seen as just bending of the body, for a better posture or exercise ... but in the East, it is a contemporary science, vitally relevant to our times.

Yogis: The term Yogi originated in ancient India and is someone who practices yoga as a holistic lifestyle and who seeks spiritual enlightenment. They are practitioners of asanas and pranayama (controlling one's breath). Known for their quality of Self-awareness they embody the principles of Yoga in all aspects of life and commit to the path of mindfulness, discipline and conscious living. The common goal is to achieve a state of harmony between body, mind and spirt.

Follow us on:
Facebook: facebook.com/ascensionforyou
or
Twitter: https://twitter.com/ascensionforyou

… and become part of our community who love
to receive uplifting messages for the heart and soul!

Want to let others know what you think?
Please make your opinion known by leaving
a 'star rating' and/or a review
at your favourite online retailer. Thank you!

www.ingramcontent.com/pod-product-compliance
Lightning Source LLC
LaVergne TN
LVHW021654060526
838200LV00050B/2351